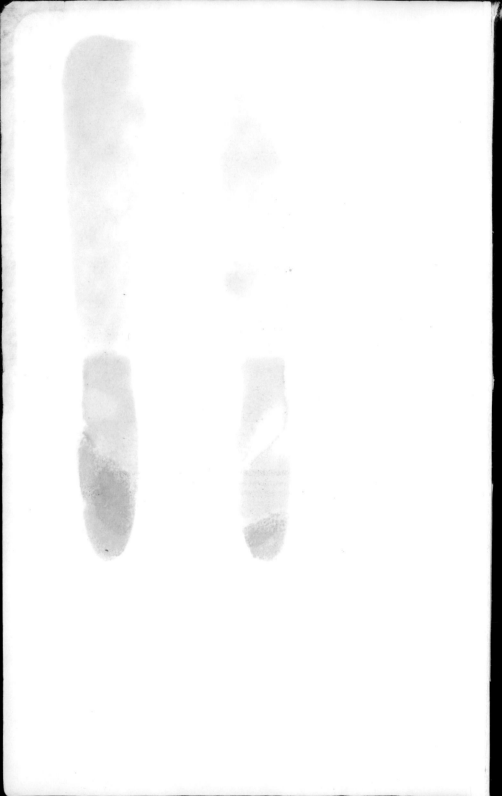

JANE AUSTEN'S
ART OF ALLUSION

Jane Austen's
Art of Allusion

KENNETH L. MOLER

UNIVERSITY OF NEBRASKA PRESS · LINCOLN

Publishers on the Plains
UNP

Part of chapter 2 of this study appeared, in an altered form, as a note entitled "*Sense and Sensibility* and Its Sources" in *The Review of English Studies*, 17 (1966): 413–419. A somewhat different version of chapter 3 appeared as "*Pride and Prejudice*: Jane Austen's 'Patrician Hero'" in *Studies in English Literature*, 7 (1967): 491–508. This material is included by permission of the editors of *The Review of English Studies* and *Studies in English Literature*.

First printing: September, 1968
Second printing: January, 1969

Manufactured in the United States of America

For Margaret Thomsen Moler

Contents

INTRODUCTION   1

1   *Northanger Abbey* and the "Young Lady's Introduction to the World"   17

2   *Sense and Sensibility* and the "Sensible Sister"   43

3   *Pride and Prejudice* and the "Patrician Hero"   75

4   *Mansfield Park* and Feminine "Accomplishments"   109

5   *Emma* and the "Formula of Romance"   155

6   *Persuasion* and "Modern Philosophy"   187

AFTERWORD   225

ACKNOWLEDGMENTS   229

INDEX   231

vii

Introduction

The following readings are attempts to discuss Jane Austen's novels in relation to eighteenth- and early nineteenth-century works, fictional and nonfictional, of the sorts that are mentioned in her letters and often referred to in her other writings. All of Jane Austen's novels contain large amounts of materials that were the common property of novelists, essayists, moralists, and other writers of her day. She alters these materials greatly, and part of the interest in studying her "borrowings" from the common stock lies in observing the skill with which various means are employed to revivify them and make them her personal possessions. Several critics have commented upon this aspect of Jane Austen's art, and I shall at times do so myself. Chiefly, however, these essays will be concerned with another aspect of her handling of the conventional. It seems to me that in each of Jane Austen's novels the manipulation of one, or perhaps a combination of several traditional motifs, character types, situations, or themes constitutes an important part of the moral and intellectual substance, the "meaning," of the work as a whole. The Austen novel consistently tends to define its vision of life in relation to literature; Jane Austen habitually expresses herself in terms of imitation, parody, correction of her predecessors and contemporaries. This tendency is a habit of mind with Jane Austen—a habit that her letters and juvenilia, saturated as they are with both comic and serious echoes of her reading, might prepare the reader to expect. It is also, I believe, an artistic strategy aimed at an audience that shared her literary milieu. The "borrowings" from the common stock are often implicit invitations to the reader to see relationships and make comparisons between her works and what they resemble; and the early nineteenth-century reader's interpretations of the novels, his sense of what they "said," would arise in part from such comparisons. The chapters to follow, then, are all based on an assumption that it is profitable to consider some of Jane Austen's "borrowings" as things more nearly akin to "allusions," implied references that she expects to affect her audience. It is impossible, of course, to recreate fully the responses of a nineteenth-century audience to Jane Austen's materials and manner of manipulating them. But treating some of her borrowings as allusions and examining their origins and associations can increase one's sensitivity to an important aspect of her art and sometimes assist in approaching the critical problems that the novels raise.[1]

My readings of Jane Austen's novels also involve some assumptions about the major intellectual preoccupations underlying her mature work, and it seems proper to acknowledge these before proceeding further. In the first place, there is what Jane Austen refers to as "self-knowledge." The attainment by one or more characters of what Edmund

---

[1] It is, I trust, clear that I do not aim at detailed coverage of all of the "borrowed" materials in Jane Austen's novels. As my footnotes will in part indicate, however, I do not mean to deny, or unduly minimize, the importance of matter other than what I concentrate on in the chapters to follow.

Bertram calls " 'the most valuable knowledge . . . the knowledge of ourselves and of our duty' " is clearly an important
concern in each novel from *Northanger Abbey* to *Persuasion*.[2]
What Jane Austen means by "self-knowledge," however,
perhaps requires some discussion. One fairly widely held
view of her meaning is ably presented in Lionel Trilling's
work on her novels. Trilling's views on the nature and
function of self-knowledge seem to have influenced several
of his writings on Jane Austen; they are most clearly
developed, however, in an essay on *Emma* in *Encounter*.[3]
As Trilling there interprets the novel, *Emma* has as one of
its main themes the modern problem of the search for
identity in a troubled, confusing modern world. According
to Trilling, the world of Highbury—the world of the
Westons, Miss Bates, Mr. Woodhouse, and Mr. Knightley—
is an idyllic, almost mythlike one in which characters are not
disturbed by the problems of the modern consciousness.
Emma, on the other hand, is a typically complex modern
character in search of her own identity. In *Emma*, Trilling
says:

> Jane Austen contrives an idyllic world, or the closest
> approximation to it that the genre of the novel will permit,
> and brings into contrast with it the actualities of the social
> world, of the modern self. In the precincts of Highbury

[2] *The Novels of Jane Austen* (London: Oxford University Press,
1933), vol. 3: *Mansfield Park*, p. 459. All subsequent references to
Jane Austen's fiction will be to the five volumes of this edition and to
the subsequent *The Works of Jane Austen* (London: Oxford University
Press, 1954), vol. 6: *Minor Works*.

[3] Lionel Trilling, "*Emma*," *Encounter*, 8 (1957): 45–59. See also
the chapter on *Mansfield Park* in Trilling's *The Opposing Self* (New
York: Viking Press, 1955), pp. 206–230, and his "A Portrait of Western
Man" in *The Listener* (June 11, 1953), pp. 969–971, 974.

there are no bad people, and no adverse judgments to be made. Only a modern critic would think to call Mr. Woodhouse an idiot and an old woman; in the novel he is called "the kind-hearted, polite old gentleman." Only Emma with her modern consciousness, comes out with it that Miss Bates is a bore, and only Emma can give herself to the thought that Mr. Weston would be a "higher character" if he were not so simple and open-hearted. It is from outside Highbury that the peculiarly modern traits of insincerity and vulgarity come, in the person of Frank Churchill and Mrs. Elton. With the exception of Emma herself, every person in Highbury lives in harmony and peace—even Mr. Elton, had Emma but let him alone!—and not merely because they are simple and undeveloped: Mr. Knightley and Mrs. Weston are no less innocent than Mr. Woodhouse and Miss Bates, and if they please us and do not bore us by a perfection of manner and feeling which is at once lofty and homely, it is because we accept the assumptions of the idyllic world which they inhabit—we have been led to believe that man may live in "harmony and peace with himself and the external world." [4]

"There is," however, "sufficient reason to be kind to Emma,"

and perhaps for nothing so much as the hope she expresses, when she first begins to understand her mistakes, that she will become, as she says, "more acquainted with herself." And, indeed, all through the novel she has sought better acquaintance with herself, not wisely, not adequately, but assiduously. How modern a quest it is, and how thoroughly it confirms Dr. Leavis's judgment that Jane Austen is the first truly modern novelist of England! ... Jane Austen, conservative and even conventional as she was, perceived

[4] Trilling, "*Emma*," p. 58.

4

the nature of the deep psychological change which accompanied the inception of democratic society—she was aware of the increase of the psychological burden of the individual, she understood the new necessity of conscious self-definition and self-criticism, of the need to make private judgments of reality. And there is no reality about which the modern person is more uncertain and more anxious than the reality of himself. For each of us, as for Emma, it is a sad, characteristic hope to become more acquainted with oneself.[5]

When Jane Austen speaks of self-knowledge in connection with Emma Woodhouse, I doubt that she has in mind something like the process of teleological self-definition, of "finding oneself," and one's relation to the world, which is the theme of many nineteenth- and twentieth-century artists. It is very difficult to find, either in Emma herself or in the opinions of the other characters in the novel, the slightest doubt about who Emma is, what she is, or why she exists. Their religion and their social organization provide Emma and her neighbors with answers to these questions. Emma Woodhouse is a child of God and a gentleman's daughter; she is the acknowledged social leader of Highbury; her duties in life are to care for her aging father and manage his household, and to assist the poor and unfortunate of her parish. These are the great, solid certainties of the book—and no one is more certain about them than Emma herself. On the contrary, has there ever been, anywhere, a character who identifies more entirely and joyfully with—and takes more advantage of—the situation in which Providence has placed him?

What is occasionally questioned in the novel—by others and eventually by Emma herself in her moments of

[5] *Ibid.*, p. 56.

5

self-knowledge—is not Emma's position or function in life, but whether something has prevented her from filling her known position properly and performing her given function well. Emma does fail to live up to her responsibilities: specifically, she fails in her duty to the unfortunate Miss Bates and Jane Fairfax, and she misuses her position in trying to wrench Harriet Smith out of her proper place in society. These are the failings for which Mr. Knightley, the voice of reason throughout the novel, reproaches Emma. After the incident at Box Hill his criticism of her is expressed explicitly in terms of her social responsibility toward Miss Bates:

> "Were she a woman of fortune, I would leave every harmless absurdity to take its chance, I would not quarrel with you for any liberties of manner. Were she your equal in situation—but, Emma, consider how far this is from being the case. She is poor; she has sunk from the comforts she was born to; and, if she lives to old age, must probably sink more. Her situation should secure your compassion. It was badly done, indeed!—You, whom she had known from an infant, whom she had seen grow up from a period when her notice was an honour, to have you now, in thoughtless spirits, and the pride of the moment, laugh at her, humble her—and before her niece, too—and before others, many of whom (certainly *some*) would be entirely guided by your treatment of her." (p. 375)

Knightley frequently tries to convince Emma that Jane Fairfax deserves her patronage (pp. 170–172, 286), and maintains as well that her treatment of Harriet Smith is improper and likely to raise the girl's ideas above her station with unfortunate results (pp. 62–63). And at the height of Emma's self-awareness, one of her major sources of remorse is the knowledge that, in spite of Knightley's admonitions, she has failed to do her obvious duty and abused the authority her position gives her:

> Oh! had she never brought Harriet forward! had she left her where she ought, and where he had told her she ought! Had she not, with a folly which no tongue could express, prevented her marrying the unexceptionable young man who would have made her happy and respectable in the line of life to which she ought to belong—all would have been safe; none of this dreadful sequel would have been. (pp. 413–414)

> Had she followed Mr. Knightley's known wishes, in paying that attention to Miss Fairfax, which was every way her due; had she tried to know her better; had she done her part towards intimacy; had she endeavoured to find a friend there instead of in Harriet Smith; she must, in all probability, have been spared from every pain which pressed on her now.—Birth, abilities, and education, had equally been marking one as an associate for her, to be received with gratitude; and the other—what was she? (p. 421)

Self-knowledge for Emma Woodhouse does not involve discovery or redefinition of the meaning of her existence; it does involve an awareness of failure in her given and accepted functions of life—and a discovery of the qualities in herself that have led to this failure.

For, in *Emma* and in Jane Austen's other novels, knowing oneself means what it had meant to a long series of classical and Christian moralists and what it means in numerous moral works of the eighteenth and early nineteenth centuries. The popular Hannah More, discussing man's faculty for "self-inspection" in her *Practical Piety* (1811), is drawing upon a long and venerable moral tradition when she

7

sees this faculty as a means of obtaining knowledge of the "interior motions" of the mind and heart:

> That deep and acute reasoner, Dr. Barrow, has remarked that "it is a peculiar excellency of human nature, and which distinguishes man from the inferior creatures more than bare reason itself, that he can reflect upon all that is done within him, can discern the tendencies of his soul. . . ."
>
> This distinguishing faculty of self-inspection would not have been conferred on man, if it had not been intended that it should be in habitual operation. . . . We have appetites to control, imaginations to restrain, tempers to regulate, passions to subdue; and how can this internal work be effected . . . how can the "little state of man" be preserved from continual insurrection, how can this restraining power be maintained if this capacity of discerning, if this faculty of inspecting be not kept in regular exercise? Without constant discipline, imagination will become an outlaw, conscience an attainted rebel.
>
> This inward eye, this power of introversion, is given us for a continual watch upon the soul. On an unremitted vigilance over its interior motions, those fruitful seeds of action, those prolific principles of vice and virtue, will depend both the formulation and the growth of our moral and religious character.[6]

According to an essay in the *Spectator* of June 7, 1712, one arrives at "a true and impartial knowledge of himself" through "the Discovery of those Vices that lurk in the secret Corners of the Soul." And for John Mason, in a treatise

[6] *The Works of Hannah More* (New York, 1884), vol. 1: *Practical Piety*, chap. 12, p. 456. All subsequent references to Hannah More's works, unless otherwise indicated, will be to this edition. For references to *Practical Piety* in Jane Austen's letters, see note 4 to chapter 4 of this study.

entitled *Self-Knowledge* (1745), an important aspect of self-knowledge is "the knowledge of the heart, the detecting and correcting hurtful prejudices, and the right government of the temper and passions."[7]

For the Austen character too, self-knowledge entails not the scanning of the universe's mysteries but "knowledge of the heart," of the "tendencies of his soul," of his human fallibility and of the particular directions in which, as an individual, he has erred and is likely to err in the complex business of the moral life. "'There is,'" for Jane Austen as for her Mr. Darcy, "'in every disposition a tendency to some particular evil, a natural defect, which not even the best education can overcome'" (*Pride and Prejudice*, p. 58). And in Emma Woodhouse's moments of crisis we find Jane Austen's heroine, not asking, "Who am I? Why was I born? What does it all mean?" but examining her tendency to a particular evil—in her case a tendency to try to twist real life into conformity with her romantic preconceptions about what life should be that has had potentially grave results for herself and those whose lives are involved with hers. After she has learned the truth about Mr. Elton's matrimonial intentions, Emma realizes that "she had taken up the idea" of Mr. Elton's marrying Harriet "and made every thing bend to it" (p. 134). And after breaking the news to Harriet, the reader is told, she "left her with every previous resolution confirmed of being humble and discreet, and repressing imagination all the rest of her life" (p. 142). At the climactic point of her story, when she asks herself, "How to understand it all?" she means, "How to understand the deceptions she had been thus practising on herself,

---

[7] John Mason, *Self-Knowledge* (Baltimore, 1832), vol. 1, chap. 1, pp. 12–13.

and living under!—The blunders, the blindness of her own
head and heart!" (pp. 411–412). "With insufferable vanity
had she believed herself in the secret of everybody's feelings;
with unpardonable arrogance proposed to arrange everybody's destiny," she learns (p. 413). This kind of self-
knowledge, this awareness of the tendencies of one's soul,
is not, to Jane Austen, a less vitally important thing, or less
difficult of attainment, than the modern self-definition of
which Trilling speaks. "Teach us to understand the sinful-
ness of our own hearts, and bring to our knowledge every
fault of temper and every evil habit in which we have
indulged to the discomfort of our fellow-creatures, and the
danger of our own souls," she used to pray, "and save us
from deceiving ourselves by pride or vanity" (*Minor
Works*, pp. 453–454). And such self-knowledge is not less
suitable as the subject matter for intricate and meaningful
art.

Another of Jane Austen's intellectual preoccupations
involves the concept of an opposition between "nature" and
"art," feeling and reason, imagination and judgment,
individual liberty and respect for established institutions,
that underlies much of the aesthetic, ethical, and political
controversy of the eighteenth and early nineteenth centuries. This concept is reflected in all of the Austen novels.
Jane Austen never comments explicitly on the issues of the
day, never produces the "critique on Walter Scott or the
history of Buonaparté" with which Cassandra was
threatened.[8] One cannot fail to note, however, her propensity

---

[8] *Jane Austen's Letters* (London: Oxford University Press, 1952),
p. 300 (February 4, 1813). All references to Jane Austen's letters will
be to this edition.

to treat characters, their development, and their relationships to one another in relation to sets of mental and temperamental oppositions, and it is clear that the tendencies of the
soul that she delights in investigating, the tendencies that
self-knowledge reveals to her characters, are generally
tendencies toward "nature" or "art" in the comprehensive
eighteenth- and early nineteenth-century uses of these
terms. This is not to say that the novels are allegories in
which some of her generation's favorite abstractions are
clothed in human form. But it is true, as many critics have
shown recently, that the complex structural patterns of her
novels, and their relevance to the intellectual currents of
Jane Austen's period, emerge most clearly when the novels
are read in the light of the antithetical patterns that entered
so deeply into the thinking of the day. In probing the souls
of her "intricate characters" she is probing the forces behind
the revolutions in thought and art of her generation.

It would seem that Jane Austen, like many of her predecessors and some of her contemporaries, generally tends
to conceive of excellence as a mean between "art" and
"nature," and to identify faults in character—as in art and
in politics—with excesses on the side of "nature" or of
"art." In her novels this habit of mind appears in a tendency
to set as the goal for her mature characters a frame of mind
which is a *concordia discors* between "art" and "nature," a
tension between the well-judging mind and the sensitive,
sympathetic heart. Dorothy Van Ghent has hit upon a good
term for describing one manifestation of this state in the
term "emotional intelligence": in Jane Austen's novels,
according to Miss Van Ghent, it is "that emotionally informed intelligence—or, shall we say, that intelligence

which informs the emotions—that we are led to look upon as desirable." [9] Self-knowledge, for the Austen protagonist, is nearly always the realization that he has allowed his heart to run away with his head, or an awareness that his value for decorum, or convention, or the prudential virtues has led him to underestimate the importance of "what throbs fast and full, though hidden, what the blood rushes through, what is the unseen seat of life and the sentient target of death." [10] Self-knowledge is not followed by a total change of personality; what is desired is that one's native propensities be balanced by an awareness of the value of quite different ones. Jane Austen, like her Anne Elliot, believes that all "qualities of the mind ... should have ... proportions and limits" (*Persuasion*, p. 116).

Finally, Jane Austen's lively sense of the difficulty of understanding human nature, and of the variety of ways in which a given action may be interpreted, must be considered. In each of the novels at least one character is made painfully aware of the difficulty of knowing other people when he learns that the ideas he had formed about the character and motivations of another person, or persons, have been almost totally wrong. Thus Catherine Morland learns that she has been deceived by Isabella Thorpe, and that she has grossly exaggerated General Tilney's ill nature. When *Sense and Sensibility* ends, Marianne Dashwood has learned that she has misunderstood her sister, Colonel Brandon, Willoughby, and many others. The plot of *Pride and Preju-*

[9] Dorothy Van Ghent, *The English Novel: Form and Function* (New York: Harper & Row, 1953), p. 107.

[10] This, of course, is what "Miss Austen ignores" according to Charlotte Brontë in the famous letter to W. S. Williams of April 12, 1850. See Clement Shorter, *The Brontës: Life and Letters* (New York: Charles Scribner's Sons, 1909), 2: 127–128.

dice turns on Elizabeth's and Darcy's learning to appreciate one another better after their initial misunderstandings. Edmund Bertram is blinded to Mary Crawford's real nature throughout most of *Mansfield Park*, just as Sir Thomas Bertram fails to see the shortcomings of his daughters and the greater worth of Fanny Price. Emma Woodhouse is deceived about almost everyone around her, and Lady Russell, in *Persuasion*, fails at first to understand Captain Wentworth.

The problem of the interpretation of character and motive is closely involved with Jane Austen's interest in self-knowledge and her preoccupation with the clash between "art" and "nature." For Jane Austen is interested not only in the variety of interpretations to which a given action is subject, but also in the preconceptions and traits of personality that cause the percipient of an action to see it as he does. Thus an Austen protagonist misunderstands another character because of certain characteristics—the "tendencies of his soul"—peculiar to the protagonist. And because Jane Austen is inclined to classify the tendencies of the soul according to the "art-nature" antithesis, the protagonist's vision is generally faulty as the result of a bias toward "nature" or "art." Marianne Dashwood is unjust to her sister and Colonel Brandon and is more than just to Willoughby because of her bias toward "sensibility." Emma Woodhouse misunderstands on a colossal scale because she tries to judge the real world by the standards of her romantic imagination. Lady Russell fails to appreciate Captain Wentworth because of her prudential bias. The Austen character's failure in moral-emotional perception is the concomitant—almost the symptom—of his failure to know himself and to be aware of his temperamental bias.

The attainment of self-knowledge is usually the result of the realization that one has failed to see another person as he really is; and it is frequently described in metaphors that suggest a recovery from a sort of moral blindness. At the climactic points of their careers Marianne Dashwood, Elizabeth Bennet, Emma Woodhouse, and other characters say, in one way or another, "I have been blinded." And the ability to perceive clearly the character and motives of another is the sign of the mind that knows itself. Self-knowledge, brought about by his family's calamities, makes Sir Thomas Bertram understand and love Fanny Price better than he has done. The recognition of her folly in judging General Tilney in terms of her youthful "visions of romance" helps Catherine Morland see through Isabella Thorpe's romantic language to the rather sordid opportunism it is meant to conceal.[11]

I do not, of course, mean to imply that Jane Austen's

[11] "Self-knowledge indeed does not enlarge or increase our natural capacities, but it guides and regulates them; leads us to the right use and application of them; and removes a great many things which obstruct their due exercise; as pride, prejudice, and passion etc., which oftentimes so miserably pervert the rational powers.

He that hath taken a just measure of himself . . . knows how to judge of men and human nature better;—for human nature, setting aside the difference of natural genius, and the improvements of education and religion, is pretty much the same in all. There are the same passions and appetites, the same natural infirmities and inclinations in all mankind; though some are more predominant and distinguishable in some than they are in others. So that, if a man be but well acquainted with his own, this, together with a very little observation on human life, will soon discover to him those of other men; and show him very impartially their particular failings and excellences, and help him to form a much truer sentiment of them than if he were to judge only by their exterior, the appearance they make in the eye of the world, or the character given of them by others." John Mason, *Self-Knowledge*, vol. 2, chap. 6, pp. 143–144.

novels can be reduced to treatises on any or all of the subjects just mentioned. I do mean to postulate the importance of the clash between "art" and "nature" and the quests for self-knowledge, as it is here defined, and a capacity for just and sympathetic interpretation of human nature, in Jane Austen's mature writing. These are concerns that influence the artistic workings of each of the novels about to be discussed, and the chapters to follow will return to them with considerable frequency.

I

Northanger Abbey and the "Young Lady's Introduction to the World"

⌒⟶

All criticism of *Northanger Abbey* must take into account the fact that the work is in part a satire, in the manner of Jane Austen's juvenilia, on the popular fiction of her day. Most obviously, Jane Austen mocks her fellow authors through the treatment of Catherine Morland as a "female Quixote" whose imagination is temporarily so disordered by novel reading that she believes General Tilney to be an English Montoni. Moreover, the entire novel is patterned as a sort of antitype to a hypothetical work that is a composite of typical novelists' materials.[1] Many readers have noted that Catherine, only moderately attractive and possessed of a mind "about as ignorant and uninformed as the female mind at seventeen usually is" (p. 18), is the antithesis of the

[1] I wish to emphasize the difference between the two kinds of satire just mentioned. In "Quixotic" satire a character absorbs misconceptions from reading a certain kind of literature; in the second sort of satire characters are not necessarily deluded by, or even aware of, the literature that they and their actions mock. Catherine Morland is treated as a mock heroine of the second type of satire consistently throughout *Northanger Abbey*. She is a "female Quixote" when, after reading Mrs. Radcliffe, she imagines Northanger Abbey to be another Udolpho—and, in my opinion, *only* then, as will become apparent later.

too-beautiful and too-accomplished Cecilias and Emmelines of the day. Henry Tilney, being neither incredibly handsome, extremely wealthy, of mysterious origin, nor even a hopeless victim of Catherine's charms from their first meeting, is well qualified for the role of a mock hero. Isabella Thorpe is a burlesque version of typical confidantes such as Fanny Burney's Miss Mirvan. Mrs. Allen is the antitype to what we might call the "bad chaperone" of fiction—the supposed protectress who, like Ann Radcliffe's Madame Cheron or Fanny Burney's Madame Duval, turns out to be a source of distress to the heroine. She might be expected to reduce Catherine to wretchedness "by her imprudence, vulgarity, or jealousy . . . by intercepting her letters, ruining her character, or turning her out of doors" (p. 20); but Mrs. Allen turns out to be nothing more than a kindly bore. General Tilney and John Thorpe are the "villains" of *Northanger Abbey*. Like Montoni, the General carries the heroine of the story off to his remote, romantic mansion, planning to dispose of her in marriage to his advantage. John Thorpe, in the manner of Fanny Burney's Mr. Monckton and other villains, "ruins the character" of the heroine by telling General Tilney that Catherine's family is poor and disreputable, and on one occasion even carries her off against her will. Even the conclusion of *Northanger Abbey* is a reversal of the novelists' traditional claims about the high moral tendencies of their works. "I leave it to be settled," Jane Austen says, "by whomsoever it may concern, whether the tendency of this work be altogether to recommend parental tyranny, or reward filial disobedience." (p. 252)[2]

[2] The rewards of parental tyranny and filial disobedience were common themes in the novels of the day. It is possible, however, that Jane Austen may have had particularly in mind the lengthy moral

One of the major problems that *Northanger Abbey* raises involves the relationship of the novel's satiric element to its other main concern—the story of Catherine Morland's development from girlhood to comparative intellectual and emotional maturity. It is generally agreed that *Northanger Abbey* tells the story of Catherine's progress toward adulthood, but there has been some diversity of opinion as to the relationship of the novel's aspect as a commentary on fiction to the theme of Catherine's growth. Some critics feel that Catherine's development *is* a commentary on the fiction of the day, and nothing more. Catherine is a subtler version of the female Quixotes of Charlotte Lennox, Eaton Stannard Barrett, and others, and her development consists primarily or exclusively in throwing off the romantic illusions derived from her reading.[3] Others hold that *Northanger Abbey* is more concerned with life than with literature, and that Catherine's female Quixotism and the treatment of her as a mock heroine are incidental, if not in fact an incumbrance, to the novel's main theme.[4]

---

summary at the conclusion of Eliza Parsons' *The Mysterious Warning* (1796), one of the novels mentioned by Isabella Thorpe in *Northanger Abbey* (p. 40). In this remarkably tedious summary Mrs. Parsons manages to attribute nearly all of the dire events that have occurred in the course of her story either to the tyranny of stubborn parents or to the disobedience of self-willed children. Jane Austen's satire is double-barreled, since, in spite of their professions to the contrary, novelists like Mrs. Parsons did in fact recommend parental tyranny —or at least make it seem necessary to romance—and, ultimately, reward filial disobedience at the fairy-tale conclusions of their stories.

[3] This is presumably the view of Howard S. Babb, in *Jane Austen's Novels: The Fabric of Dialogue* (Columbus: Ohio State University Press, 1962), pp. 86–87, and of Cynthia Griffin in "The Development of Realism in Jane Austen's Early Novels," *ELH*, 30 (1963): 36–52.

[4] See, for example, the discussion of *Northanger Abbey* in Mary Lascelles' *Jane Austen and her Art* (London: Oxford University Press, 1939), pp. 59–64.

It is surely a mistake to see Catherine only as a female Quixote. Novel reading is really made responsible only for Catherine's folly during her stay at Northanger Abbey. The rest of her errors are due simply to her general mental immaturity. Her most serious error—her attachment to Isabella Thorpe and blindness to Isabella's real nature—occurs chiefly *before* Catherine has been introduced to the works of the day. The " 'new books' " of the period, she tells Isabella, " 'do not come in our way' " at her father's house; until her friendship with Isabella she has not, to the reader's knowledge, read any novel other than *Sir Charles Grandison* (p. 41). Her initial difficulty in grasping the real nature of John Thorpe is certainly not due to associating him with a figure in romance. And when the "visions of romance" acquired from her reading have been dispelled by Henry Tilney, and Catherine's role as a female Quixote terminated, she is still having some difficulties in understanding human nature similar to those she experienced at the beginning of the story. She is nearly as bewildered by General Tilney's hypocrisy toward the end of the novel as she had been by John Thorpe's lies at the beginning of her career. She can still be thrown into confusion when she learns that, in spite of the General's declaration that Henry need not make any special preparations to entertain the party from Northanger at his parsonage, Henry must leave Northanger two days earlier than he had intended in order to do just that:

> The inexplicability of the General's conduct dwelt much in her thoughts . . . why he should say one thing so positively, and mean another all the while, was most unaccountable! How were people, at that rate, to be understood? (p. 211)

Female Quixotism is only a temporary aspect of Catherine's general naïveté.

As I shall indicate later, I must agree in general with those critics who consider *Northanger Abbey* an immature and not very unified work in which satire of fiction often tends to interfere with more important business. Catherine's adventures as a female Quixote mar the credibility of the more realistic "serious" story of her development into maturity, and the patterning of *Northanger Abbey* as a typical novel of the period in reverse seems to lead Jane Austen astray toward the end of the novel. On the other hand, the novel's satiric element, while not well integrated with the story of Catherine's development, is in some respects a little more nearly related to it than one might at first think. For one of the fictional motifs that Jane Austen borrows for satire also functions, in another way, within the story of Catherine's growth, becoming as Jane Austen manipulates it a commentary on, a way of seeing, Catherine's story. And if one reads the novel in terms of Jane Austen's handling of this motif, he can glimpse certain other relationships, albeit not particularly fortunate ones, between the satire and the "serious" story of *Northanger Abbey*. The motif, best known as it appears in the novels of Fanny Burney, but popular with many other writers as well, might be called the motif of the "young lady's introduction to the world"; and some discussion of it is in order.

I

The exposure of youth to the ways of the world was a favorite theme in eighteenth-century literature; the progeny of Tom Jones, male and female, were no less numerous than Pamela's daughters. The popularity of the theme was due in part to the fact that it was seen as an expression of one of the most important and pervasive intellectual issues of the period, the antithesis between "nature" and "art," feeling and reason, imagination and judgment, benevolence and prudence. The distinguishing characteristic of youth, according to many writers of the period, is a benevolence that paints all the world in rosy hues not its own. Warm-hearted and naturally virtuous themselves (unless they have been corrupted by excessively worldly upbringings or some other kind of misfortune), young people assume that everyone is similar to them. "When first we enter on the theatre of the world," says Mrs. Radcliffe in *The Castles of Athlin and Dunbayne* (1789),

> ... the young imagination heightens every scene, and the warm heart expands to all around it. The happy benevolence of our feelings prompts us to believe that every body is good, and excites our wonder why every body is not happy. ... As we advance in life, imagination is compelled to relinquish a part of her sweet delirium: we are led reluctantly to truth through the paths of experience; and the objects of our fond attention are viewed with a severer eye. Here an altered scene appears;—frowns where late were smiles; deep shades where late was sunshine: mean passions, or disgusting apathy, stain the features of the principal figures. We turn indignant from a prospect so miserable, and court again the sweet illusions of our early days; but ah! they are fled for ever! [5]

Their naïve benevolence can lead the young to displays of imprudence and poor judgment when they first enter "the world." Their feelings, however, are always amiable ones;

[5] Ann Radcliffe, *The Castles of Athlin and Dunbayne* (London, 1811), pp. 4–5. This kind of wistful reflection on the beautiful lost illusions of youth is extremely common in the literature of the period.

and like the "noble savage" and other sorts of primitives of the period, the naïve young person in eighteenth- and early nineteenth-century literature is often a reproach to the folly and vice of the sophisticated society into which he is introduced.

Fanny Burney's heroines are clearly among the female descendants of Tom Jones. In *Evelina* "a young female, educated in the most secluded retirement, makes, at the age of seventeen, her first appearance upon the great and busy stage of life." [6] In her innocence Evelina assumes that everyone she meets is as simple and virtuous as she herself is. As Mr. Villars, her guardian, describes his ward "her guileless and innocent soul fancied all the world to be pure and disinterested as herself, and . . . her heart was open to every impression with which love, pity, or art might assail it" (p. 140). Her lack of experience leads to some errors: "with a virtuous mind, a cultivated understanding, a feeling heart, ignorance of the forms, and inexperience in the manners, of the world, occasion all the little incidents which this volume records" (p. 10). There is little doubt, however, that she is superior to most of the more sophisticated characters in the novel. Similar situations are found in *Camilla* and, to a lesser extent, in *Cecilia*. Cecilia is exposed to London life after a childhood spent in simpler surroundings and is bewildered because of a lack of worldly wisdom. And lack of experience is responsible for the errors into which the warmhearted Camilla falls:

> foresight, the offspring of Judgment, or the disciple of Experience, made no part of the character of Camilla,

[6] Fanny Burney, *Evelina* (Garden City, New York: Doubleday & Co., n.d.), pp. 9–10. All subsequent references are to this edition.

whose impetuous disposition was open to every danger of indiscretion, though her genuine love of virtue glowed warm with juvenile ardour.[7]

Fanny Burney, like Fielding, emphasizes the need for her young people to acquire "art" in addition to their natural benevolence. In the course of her career the Burneyan heroine acquires experience and polish, meets with favor in the eyes of a society figure, an attractive and eminently eligible young man, and ultimately is rewarded with his hand. Other novelists of the period adapted the motif of the young lady's introduction to suit different beliefs and temperaments. In the hands of writers more strongly influenced by the romantic primitivism of the period "the world" is rejected in disgust by the sensitive soul. The father of Emily St. Aubert in *The Mysteries of Udolpho* has retired to his country estate, a disillusioned man, after his introduction to the world. He, the reader is told,

> had known life in other forms than that of pastoral simplicity, having mingled in the gay and busy scenes of the world; but the flattering portrait of mankind, which his heart had delineated in early youth his experience had too sorrowfully corrected . . . he retired from the multitude "More in pity than in anger," to the scenes of simple nature, to the pure delights of literature, and to the domestic virtues.[8]

And in the story of Emily, Mrs. Radcliffe employs the materials of the "introduction" motif chiefly as a means of denouncing sophisticated society. Emily, like Evelina, is

[7] Fanny Burney, *Camilla* (London, 1796), vol. 2, bk. 2, chap. 7, p. 137.

[8] Ann Radcliffe, *The Mysteries of Udolpho* (London, 1794), vol. 1, chap. 1, p. 2.

brought up in the country. She is introduced to society under the chaperonage of her worldly aunt. But her encounter with "the world" is primarily a means by which the corruptions of society may be contrasted with the elegant simplicity of her life in the country with her father, and the primitive virtues of the rustics with whom she resides in the Pyrenees.

The motif is popular with numerous authors of even less distinction. It is the major organizing force in Agnes Maria Bennet's *Ellen, Countess of Castle Howell* (1794), for instance, where the heroine, who has been brought up in a ruined castle in the wilds of Wales, is taken to London when she marries. Ignored by her husband, and inadequately chaperoned by his two foolish aunts, she is left to her own devices amid the brilliant scenes of dissipation that London provides. As a result of her ingenuousness and impulsiveness, and the machinations of a London rake, the innocent Ellen's reputation is compromised, and her husband leaves her. A happy ending is in store, but only after Ellen's ignorance of the ways of the world has caused considerable distress. The "introduction" motif crops up in Elizabeth Helme's *Duncan and Peggy* (1794), where Peggy is exposed to fashionable society by the worldly Lady Beugle; in Harriet Smith's favorite, Regina Maria Roche's *The Children of the Abbey* (1798), when Amanda Fitzallen is taken to London by an evil sophisticate named Lady Greystock; and in countless other novels of the period as well. Clearly, it was familiar material to Jane Austen's audience.[9]

9 As F. W. Bradbrook points out in *Jane Austen and Her Predecessors* (Cambridge: Cambridge University Press, 1966), p. 16, Dr. Johnson discusses the expectations of a young lady about to enter "the world" in the *Idler*, 80 (October 27, 1759).

Evidence that Jane Austen was aware of the prevalence of the introduction motif is found in her juvenilia, where she singles it out for satire. In "Letter the First" from "A Collection of Letters," the exaggerated displays of parental anxiety with which the typical "young lady" is dispatched on her career are held up to ridicule. A mother agitatedly describes her daughters' "entrée into Life"—an event which takes the form of a teatime visit to one of their neighbors and her daughter. "As the moment approached for our departure," she writes,

> you can have no idea how the sweet Creatures trembled with fear and expectation.... I ... thus addressed them. "My dear Girls the moment is now arrived when I am to reap the rewards of all my Anxieties and Labours towards you during your Education. You are this Evening to enter a World in which you will meet with many wonderful Things; Yet let me warn you against suffering yourselves to be meanly swayed by the Follies and Vices of others, for believe me my beloved Children if you do—I shall be very sorry for it." They both assured me that they would ever remember my advice with Gratitude, and follow it with attention; That they were prepared to find a World full of things to amaze and shock them: but that they trusted their behaviour would never give me reason to repent the Watchful Care with which I had presided over their infancy and formed their Minds—" ... When we arrived at Warleigh, poor Augusta could scarcely breathe, while Margaret was all Life and Rapture. "The long-expected Moment is now arrived (said she) and we shall soon be in the World."—In a few Moments we were in Mrs. Cope's parlour.... Imagine my dear Madam how delighted I must have been in beholding as I did, how attentively they observed every object they saw, how disgusted with some

Things, how enchanted with others, how astonished at all! On the whole however they returned in raptures with the World, its Inhabitants, and Manners. (*Minor Works*, pp. 151–152)

One is reminded of the verbose anxiety of Mr. Villars, in *Evelina*, and of the pages of advice which follow Evelina to London. The popular motif, along with other features of the novels of the day, is also satirized in *Northanger Abbey*. Catherine's first appearance at the Upper Rooms is laughingly referred to as "our heroine's entrée into life" (p. 20). As noted earlier, Mrs. Allen is introduced as a burlesque version of the "young lady's" inadequate chaperone. When Catherine is about to set off on her adventures, Jane Austen humorously expects that Mrs. Morland will be full of salutary advice and dire premonitions. "When the hour of departure drew near," she says,

> the maternal anxiety of Mrs. Morland will be naturally supposed to be most severe. A thousand alarming presentiments of evil to her beloved Catherine from this terrific separation must oppress her heart with sadness, and drown her in tears for the last day or two of their being together; and advice of the most important and applicable nature must of course flow from her wise lips in their parting conference in her closet. Cautions against the violence of such noblemen and baronets as delight in forcing young ladies away to some remote farm-house, must, at such a moment, relieve the fulness of her heart. (p. 18)

Unfortunately, however,

> Mrs. Morland knew so little of lords and baronets, that she entertained no notion of their general mischievousness, and was wholly unsuspicious of danger to her daughter from their machinations. Her cautions were confined to the

27

following points. "I beg, Catherine, you will always wrap yourself up very warm about the throat, when you come from the Rooms at night; and I wish you would try to keep some account of the money you spend;—I will give you this little book on purpose." (pp. 18–19)

II

But in *Northanger Abbey* Jane Austen does something more than satirize the motif of the young lady's introduction to the world. Her early nineteenth-century audience would easily perceive that she also uses it as the foundation for her "serious" study of Catherine Morland's development. The story of Catherine's growth recalls, quite consistently, the pattern of the young lady's introduction to the world as it was developed by Fanny Burney and other novelists of the period.[10] Catherine, like Evelina, is brought up "in the most secluded retirement" at a country rectory. When she arrives at Bath she is a child of nature, and naturally good. "'Open, candid, artless, guileless, forming no pretensions and knowing no disguise,'"[11] she enters the world "'looking forward to pleasures untasted and unalloyed, and free from the apprehension of evil as from the knowledge of it'" (p. 237). Full of naïve illusions, she is introduced to the mystifying world of Bath. Mrs. Allen—a genuine "bad chaperone" in her way as well as a burlesque figure—is unable to advise her even in so simple a matter as the question of whether she

[10] In *The Women Novelists* (London: W. Collins & Sons, 1918), p. 92, R. Brimley Johnson also discusses the close relationship between *Northanger Abbey* and *Evelina*.

[11] *Northanger Abbey*, p. 206. Henry Tilney originally uses the words sarcastically, to describe Isabella Thorpe, but his sister makes their application to Catherine quite clear.

should go riding with John Thorpe. And Catherine, left to her own devices, displays her innocence at every turn, painfully acquires a better knowledge of the world, and ultimately marries a young man who, in the manner of Fanny Burney's heroes, has supervised her progress.

Most of Catherine's problems arise from the same cause that is responsible for the troubles of other "young ladies" of the period. Having no other basis for judgment, she consistently estimates character and motive solely in terms of her own warmth and sincerity. " 'How very little trouble it can give you to understand the motive of other people's actions,'" Henry Tilney says to her:

> "With you, it is not, How is such a one likely to be influenced? What is the inducement most likely to act upon such a person's feelings, age, situation, and probable habits of life considered?—but, how should *I* be influenced, what would be *my* inducement in acting so and so?" (p. 132)

Accustomed only to the society of people who are as open-hearted and literalminded as herself, she cannot deal with, or even recognize, anything that approaches evil or insincerity. It is for this reason that she does not know what to make of John Thorpe's boasts and lies,

> for she had not been brought up to understand the propensities of a rattle, nor to know to how many idle assertions and impudent falsehoods the excess of vanity will lead. Her own family were plain, matter of fact people, who seldom aimed at wit of any kind; her father, at the utmost, being contented with a pun, and her mother with a proverb; they were not in the habit therefore of telling lies to increase their importance, or of asserting at one moment what they would contradict the next. (pp. 65–66)

29

Even the "archness and pleasantry" of Henry Tilney's conversation are "hardly understood by her" because she does not know whether his statements are to be taken literally. She cannot comprehend the duplicity and heartlessness of Captain Tilney until they are demonstrated beyond all possibility of doubt. And, most important of all, she is completely taken in by Isabella Thorpe's hypocritical professions of love for her brother and friendship for herself. Because she judges Isabella in terms of her own warmhearted guilelessness, she is blinded to her real nature. She resists, almost wilfully, the insight into her character which the contradictions between Isabella's professions and her practice are continually affording.

As is the case with other primitives of the period, Catherine's innocence and goodness are a reproach to the duplicity, vanity, and self-seeking of many of the more sophisticated characters in her story. Even when she is duped she is superior to her deceivers, and the extent to which she serves as a vehicle for satire on the actual society of the period as well as the world of fiction is not always appreciated as it should be. But Jane Austen insists, as Fielding and Fanny Burney do, that her central character add a degree of "art" to her natural goodness. In the course of her introduction to the world Catherine is made aware of the fact that her naïve vision of things is an impairment of her moral perception, and develops a more mature approach to life. It is not long before she begins to understand John Thorpe, different as he is from herself, and to dislike him as she ought. And although she does not progress far enough during her stay at Bath to penetrate Isabella Thorpe's façade completely, she does venture on occasion to question Isabella's perfection. Her adventures at Northanger Abbey constitute a further phase in her development as she learns important lessons about herself and others with the help of her mentor-lover Henry Tilney.[12]

III

Before the final stage of Catherine's development is completed, however, something else occurs. In the chapters that deal with the adventures at Northanger Abbey, although Jane Austen continues to employ the motif of the young lady's introduction to the world, she employs it in a new way. Catherine's Quixotic behavior at Northanger is used to turn the "introduction" motif upon the novelists from whom Jane Austen borrows it and to sharply dissociate her moral vision from theirs. When she sets out for Northanger, Catherine has in part corrected her youthful naïveté: she now realizes that everyone is not so good and sincere as she is. But she has been "introduced" to evil and duplicity in another way, through the introduction to life that her novel reading has provided. The reader soon sees, however, that her reading leads her to a view of human nature that is only a little less oversimplified than that with which Catherine made her entrance into society: she merely moves from the illusions of total inexperience to another, less severe, form of moral blindness that Jane Austen calls "the

[12] For a different account of the novel's tendency to fall into "Bath" and "Northanger" episodes see C. S. Emden, "*Northanger Abbey* Re-Dated," *Notes and Queries*, 195 (1950): 407–410. Emden feels that the "Gothic" occurrences at Northanger were added at a later date to a "light satire of manners comprising occasional burlesque of the silly sentimental novel . . . written in 1794." His theory seems to assume a greater sensitivity to distinctions between Gothic and other kinds of fiction on the parts of Jane Austen and her contemporaries than I believe existed.

visions of romance." The novels that Catherine reads certainly contain a full measure of evil; but as Jane Austen shows, they treat character as a matter of black and white: all who are not shining heroines and heroes are villains of the deepest dye, Montonis and Moncktons.[13] It is with this kind of moral vision that Catherine approaches General Tilney. It is obvious even to Catherine that the General is not what he would have her believe he is. In spite of his amiable behavior to her, it is apparent that his own children are wary of him. In spite of the fact that he declares himself to be entirely at Catherine's disposal, he contrives to postpone the tour of the abbey for which she is so anxious. But instead of seeing General Tilney as he really is—as a bad-tempered man whose determination to have his own way overcomes even his desire to make a favorable impression on the girl to whom he hopes to marry his son—she magnifies his ill nature and disingenuousness until in her eyes he assumes the stature of a fictional villain. He is unwilling to show the abbey because of the horrid mysteries concealed there. He is moody because he is tortured by a guilty conscience. And Catherine sets out to uncover the secret of the abbey.

The disappointment of her expectations and the interview with Henry Tilney on the stairs take Catherine another step toward moral clear-sightedness. Henry Tilney proves

[13] In the passage in which the false vision of Jane Austen's fellow novelists is censured (*Northanger Abbey*, p. 200), only the works of Mrs. Radcliffe are mentioned. But, as her frequent satire of Fanny Burney throughout the novel indicates, the remarks are applicable, in a lesser degree, to Fanny Burney as well as to Mrs. Radcliffe. Mrs. Radcliffe is chosen as an extreme example of tendencies of which Jane Austen disapproves.

that the view of life presented in her favorite reading matter is not a trustworthy basis for judging character and motive:

> "What have you been judging from? Remember the country and the age in which we live. Remember that we are English, that we are Christians. Consult your own understanding, your own sense of the probable, your own observation of what is passing around you—Does our education prepare us for such atrocities? Do our laws connive at them? Could they be perpetrated without being known, in a country like this, where social and literary intercourse is on such a footing; where every man is surrounded by a neighborhood of voluntary spies, and where roads and newspapers lay everything open? Dearest Miss Morland, what ideas have you been admitting?" (pp. 197–198) [14]

Catherine confesses to her moral blindness:

> The visions of romance were over. Catherine was completely awakened. Henry's address, short as it had been, had more thoroughly opened her eyes to the extravagance of her late fancies than all their several disappointments had done . . . it had all been a voluntary, self-created delusion, each trifling circumstance receiving importance from an imagination resolved on alarm, and every thing forced to bend to one purpose by a mind which, before she entered the Abbey, had been craving to be frightened. (pp. 199–200)

She learns that the black and white vision of life that she has entertained is an oversimplification, a distortion of

[14] Compare A. Walton Litz, *Jane Austen: A Study of Her Artistic Development* (New York: Oxford University Press, 1965), pp. 63–68, where this and a similar passage are interpreted as signs of a tendency on Jane Austen's part to defend, as well as attack, Catherine's romantic vision.

reality. Human nature, she begins to realize, is a complex mixture of good and bad. The race is composed not of extremes but of "mixed" characters:

> Among the Alps and Pyrenees, perhaps, there were no mixed characters. There, such as were not spotless as an angel, might have the disposition of a fiend. But in England it was not so; among the English, she believed, in their hearts and habits, there was a general though unequal mixture of good and bad. Upon this conviction she would not be surprised if even in Henry and Eleanor Tilney, some slight imperfection might hereafter appear; and upon this conviction she need not fear to acknowledge some actual specks in the character of their father, who, though cleared from the grossly injurious suspicions which she must ever blush to have entertained, she did believe, upon consideration, to be not perfectly amiable. Her mind made up on these several points, and her resolution formed, of always judging and acting in future with the greatest good sense, she had nothing to do but to forgive herself, and be happier than ever. (pp. 200–201)

The lesson that Catherine's self-knowledge and her particular brand of introduction to the world have taught her is that human nature is complex and difficult to understand. Neither the naïve vision of youth—"'how should I be influenced'"—nor the black and white, adolescent "vision of romance" is a sufficient basis for the estimation of character and motive. One must judge, not on the basis of preconceptions about human nature, but on the basis of clear-sighted "'observation of what is passing around you,'" on the basis of evidence and probability. "'How is such a one likely to be influenced? What is the inducement likely to act upon such a person's feelings, age, situation, and probable habits of life considered?'"—These are the kinds of questions one must ask oneself before making judgments.

Catherine's reaction to the news of the dissolution of the engagement between Isabella Thorpe and her brother is a sign of her progress toward maturity. For, instead of judging in terms of the preconceptions of naïveté or noveldom, Catherine looks at the evidence before her and sees Isabella, at last, as she really is. When James Morland's letter arrives, Catherine at first assumes that Isabella has merely been fickle: "'Could you have believed there had been such inconstancy and fickleness, and every thing that is bad in the World?'" (p. 204). But with a little prodding from Henry Tilney she is able to see, judging on the basis of her own observation, that Isabella has been all along a coldhearted schemer, alert for the main chance. "'Now she has really got the man she likes,'" Catherine says to Henry, "'she may be constant.'" And Henry replies: "'Indeed I am afraid she will, . . . I am afraid she will be very constant, unless a baronet should come in her way; that is Frederick's only chance.—I will get the Bath paper, and look over the arrivals.'" "'You think it is all for ambition then?'" Catherine says:

> "—And, upon my word, there are some things that seem very like it. I cannot forget, that, when she first knew what my father would do for them, she seemed quite disappointed that it was not more. I never was so deceived in any one's character in my life before." (p. 206)

When Isabella, relying on Catherine's naïveté, tries to persuade her that the whole affair has simply been a misunderstanding and that she really loves John, Catherine is no longer to be taken in. Previously, she would have accepted Isabella's letter at its face value. Now, however,

> Its inconsistencies, contradictions, and falsehood, struck her from the very first. . . . "So much for Isabella," she cried, "and for all our intimacy! She must think me an idiot, or she could not have written so; but perhaps this has served to make her character better known to me than mine is to her. I see what she has been about." (p. 218)

Catherine, of course, does not realize that she has ever been the "idiot" that Isabella takes her for. But the truth of the matter is that in the course of her introduction to the world, Catherine has done a considerable amount of very necessary growing up.

A knowledge of her limitations as a judge of character and an increased insight into human nature neither provide Catherine with an infallible key to the interpretation of character nor totally do away with her naïveté. The "tendencies of her soul" remain much the same as they have always been. She still tends to view people in terms of her own personality; the assumption that they are as straightforward and good as she herself is remains the basis on which she deals with them. And when her assumptions are proven wrong, with the harshness of youth she exaggerates the viciousness of actions which do not meet her own standards. She is bewildered by General Tilney's maneuverings; and when she learns that the General had cultivated her largely in the hope of making an advantageous match for his son, she considers his actions as villainy of the deepest dye, feeling "that in suspecting General Tilney of either murdering or shutting up his wife, she had scarcely sinned against his character, or magnified his cruelty" (p. 247). But though she is still very young, Catherine has taken the Austen heroine's first steps on the road to mature womanhood. She is conscious of the possibilities of error in the complex business of moral discernment, and prepared to submit her favorite preconceptions to the test of experience.

The motif of the young lady's introduction to the world, then, in addition to being a target for Jane Austen's satire, also becomes the foundation upon which the story of Catherine Morland's growth is built. And it is by means of her handling of the motif—by following it rather closely up to a point and then employing the satiric Quixotic episodes at Northanger Abbey to make her heroine's story an "introduction" with a difference—that Jane Austen defines the nature of her heroine's moral growth. Catherine Morland progresses from a youthful "natural" innocence, identified as that of the Burneyan young lady, to what Jane Austen considers an oversimplified "black and white" moral vision which, ironically, is also identified by its resemblance to that of the novelists from whom the "introduction" motif is borrowed. Catherine then goes a step beyond this vision to an approximation of the more complex and subtle conception of human nature that is her author's. This kind of definition by allusion and contrast would not have gone unnoticed by an audience that shared Jane Austen's literary background and could see Catherine's story as an "introduction" with significant, and delightfully ironic, differences. And related, though increasingly more refined, uses of material borrowed from the literature of her day are characteristic also of her later novels.

Some qualification is necessary for what has previously been presented as a somewhat too attractive picture of

Northanger Abbey as a work in which satire and the "serious" story of Catherine Morland's development cooperate. In some ways the story of Catherine's development is seriously compromised by the novel's satiric element. In the first place the female Quixotism that Catherine displays at Northanger, although made to function in the story of Catherine's growth as a means of "definition by contrast" nevertheless remains a crude one, one that renders the story itself improbable. A total disordering of the imagination by novel reading is acceptable as a convention for satire, but it is poor motivation for a realistically developed character. It is difficult to believe that anyone, even Catherine Morland, could accept *The Mysteries of Udolpho* as a faithful picture of life and be led by it to believe a respectable English gentleman capable of the deeds of a Montoni. In later novels, instead of reducing her characters to the pasteboard creations of satire, Jane Austen employs more refined means to attain her ends; had *Northanger Abbey*'s strong orientation toward specific satire of Mrs. Radcliffe not militated against it, she might have done so here.

Moreover, the concluding chapters of the novel, in which General Tilney's violent behavior is introduced, seem to raise serious problems. The General's behavior fills out the novel's pattern of incidents derived from fiction: he suddenly and inexplicably decides to expel Catherine from Northager, just as Montoni, for instance, decided to remove Emily St. Aubert from Udolpho; and he becomes reminiscent of the inflexible parents, unalterably opposed to their children's matrimonial choices, in which the novels of the period abounded. But the violence of his behavior does not accord with the lessons Catherine's introduction to the world has taught her about the "mixed" nature of people. He comes uncomfortably close to being the unmitigated villain she originally thought him.

It is possible, of course, to assume that this was Jane Austen's intention, and to interpret the General's behavior as a bit of subtle irony on her part. After criticizing Catherine's fallacious ideas, she turns her irony also on the common sense and worldly wisdom that Henry Tilney has continually opposed to Catherine's notions. The reader is shown that "we cannot apprehend the real world by good sense alone. Good sense, ironically, is limited too." [15] A theory that attributes such subtlety to the novel is appealing. Moreover, such an ironic reversal would certainly not be uncharacteristic of Jane Austen, as some of the chapters to follow perhaps help to point out. I am unable, however, to accept this interpretation of *Northanger Abbey*. To begin with, General Tilney's behavior does not lead to an acknowledgment by Henry that his commonsensical view of

[15] Andrew H. Wright, *Jane Austen's Novels: A Study in Structure* (London: Chatto & Windus, 1954), p. 96. In his fine discussion of the novel Wright holds that the satiric element and the "serious" story of *Northanger Abbey* often undermine one another, but he uses General Tilney's actions toward the end of the book to support his contention that Catherine both acquires common sense and learns its limitations. For other interpretations holding that Catherine's "illusions" regarding the General turn out to be less illusory than the reader expects them to be, see John K. Mathison, "*Northanger Abbey* and Jane Austen's Conception of the Value of Fiction," *ELH*, 24 (1951): 138–152; Lionel Trilling, *The Opposing Self*, p. 217; Frank J. Kearful, "Satire and the Form of the Novel: The Problem of Aesthetic Unity in *Northanger Abbey*," *ELH*, 32 (1965): 511–527; and the relevant chapters in Henrietta Ten Harmsel's *Jane Austen: A Study in Fictional Conventions* (The Hague: Mouton & Co., 1964) and A. Walton Litz' *Jane Austen . . . Her Artistic Development*. (Litz does not, apparently, see General Tilney's actions as an indication that Jane Austen undermines Henry Tilney's position in the novel's moral scheme: he does cite them as signs of a partial defense of Catherine.)

life has limitations. There is, in fact, no scene in the novel in which serious failings of any kind are acknowledged by or attributed to Henry. (Catherine's flaws in judgment, on the other hand, are most explicitly acknowledged.) This, perhaps, need not prove too troublesome: Jane Austen, as her *Letters* show, expects her readers to bring "a great deal of ingenuity" to her works. But are there even hints in the novel for the reader's ingenuity to work upon, as far as the matter in question is concerned? There does not seem to be the slightest indication that the general's conduct is designed to undermine the novel's assertion that common sense such as Henry's leads to the maximum possible amount of clearsightedness. Henry is mortified by his father's actions, but it is never suggested that they reveal anything about General Tilney of which he was not aware previously. Can it come as a surprise to Henry that his father is mercenary and exceedingly ill-tempered?

This is not to say that *Northanger Abbey* is a work in which the values for which Catherine stands are rejected absolutely in favor of other ones. Obviously Catherine, even before her particular variety of introduction to the world is completed, is the most attractive character in the novel. Obviously, as was suggested earlier, she in her innocence is a reproach to certain aspects of the sophisticated world around her. Her mental outlook is not to be replaced by the worldly wisdom of an Isabella Thorpe or a General Tilney; it is a combination of Catherine's benevolence with prudence that Jane Austen favors. But she does not use General Tilney's behavior to advocate the desired blend. Mary Lascelles rightly concludes that "the burlesque element in *Northanger Abbey* has a pretty intricacy and variety. Its strands are ingeniously interwoven with one another—but not so well woven into the rest of the fabric." [16] Catherine Morland is two distinct characters. She is a vehicle (albeit a particularly delightful one) designed to satirize fiction, who resembles some of the characters in Jane Austen's juvenilia. And, in the manner of Jane Austen's more mature work, she is a human being interesting in her own right whose relationship to a fictional motif lends her additional significance. *Northanger Abbey* looks in two directions simultaneously: it is at once the most brilliant piece of Jane Austen's juvenilia, and the least satisfactory of her mature works.

[16] Mary Lascelles, *Jane Austen and Her Art*, p. 64.

2

Sense and Sensibility and the "Sensible Sister"

For all its faults, *Northanger Abbey* remains a minor favorite with Jane Austen's readers; *Sense and Sensibility* is one of the least popular of her works. Readers rather often are inclined to feel that the novel's treatment of the eighteenth-century "reason-feeling" dichotomy becomes stiff and one-sided, to object to what seems to them to be an undue preference on Jane Austen's part for the rational, cautious, conventional Elinor Dashwood and an unfair treatment of her sensitive and impetuous sister. "Marianne Dashwood . . . has been betrayed," Marvin Mudrick declares at the conclusion of a discussion of *Sense and Sensibility*, "and not by Willoughby."[1] And while few readers are as vehement in their criticisms of *Sense and Sensibility* as Mr. Mudrick is, certainly some would agree that his statement is not entirely without justification.

[1] Marvin Mudrick, *Jane Austen: Irony as Defense and Discovery* (Princeton: Princeton University Press, 1952), p. 93. Assuming that Elinor represents the moral norm of the novel, Mudrick accuses Jane Austen of frigid and insincere moralizing and inconsistency. For more moderate adverse criticism of the novel see the relevant chapter of A. Walton Litz, *Jane Austen . . . Her Artistic Development*.

But is the novel really so one-sided in its intentions, so fully committed to Elinor's prudence and rationality? I believe that Jane Austen adopts, and expects her reader in the course of the novel to develop, an ironic (though not unsympathetic) attitude toward Elinor's "sense" as well as toward Marianne's "sensibility." Perhaps she was not conscious of all the things about her "sense" heroine to which a modern reader might take exception. But she saw, and expected her readers to see, some flaws in Elinor's view of life. It is much more difficult to trace Elinor's faults than it is to perceive Marianne's errors. Much of the story of *Sense and Sensibility* is told from Elinor's point of view, and one suspects that when Jane Austen wrote the novel she was not confident enough in her powers to entrust the telling of her tale to a highly fallible character, as she did with such success in *Pride and Prejudice* and *Emma*.[2] Nevertheless, it is possible to show that she treats Elinor's brand of "sense" in a more complex fashion than is sometimes supposed.

When one considers *Sense and Sensibility* in terms of the problem of moral blindness and self-knowledge, it is obvious that Marianne Dashwood is the novel's prime candidate for the kind of moral eye-opening that Jane Austen is so fond of dealing with. The reader is in no danger of failing to note the "injustice to which [Marianne] was often led in her opinion of others, by the irritable refinement of her own mind, and the too great importance placed by her on the delicacies of a strong sensibility, and the graces of a polished manner" (pp. 201–202). She hastily concludes that, because Colonel Brandon lacks Willoughby's warmth and grace, "'he has neither genius, taste nor spirit ... his understanding

[2] The point is made by Howard Babb, *The Fabric of Dialogue*, pp. 54–55.

has no brilliancy, his feelings no ardour, and his voice no expression'" (p. 51). She is unduly contemptuous of the kindhearted, sensible, but not very refined Mrs. Jennings. She fails to do justice to Elinor's feelings because they are not vented as frequently or as noisily as her own. And she deceives herself about Willoughby because he seems to suit her romantic notions so perfectly. Serious illness, brought about by her own folly, leads Marianne to "calm and serious reflection" and to self-knowledge, and she becomes aware of her shortcomings. Her conduct before the illness, she tells Elinor after she has recovered, had been "'nothing but a series of imprudence towards myself, and want of kindness to others'":

> "Every body seemed injured by me. The kindness, the unceasing kindness of Mrs. Jennings, I had repaid with ungrateful contempt. To the Middletons, the Palmers, the Steeles, to every common acquaintance even, I had been insolent and unjust; with an heart hardened against their merits, and a temper irritated by their very attention.—To John, to Fanny,—yes, even to them, little as they deserve, I had given less than their due. But you,—you above all, above my mother had been wronged by me. I, and only I, knew your heart and its sorrows; yet, to what did it influence me? not to any compassion that could benefit you or myself . . . not less when I knew you to be unhappy, than when I believed you at ease, did I turn away from every exertion of duty or friendship; scarcely allowing sorrow to exist but with me, and leaving you, for whom I professed an unbounded affection, to be miserable for my sake."
> (p. 346)

Elinor, as noted previously, is never so obviously wrong as her sister is. Nevertheless, it can be shown that Jane Austen tries—not altogether successfully—to show that

Elinor carries her "sense" to an excess that makes her, too, a victim of moral-emotional blindness, and that significant changes in Elinor's mental outlook take place in the course of the novel.[3] Considering the relationship of Elinor and her story to some of their literary antecedents helps to make it clear that *Sense and Sensibility*, while it may be artistically unsuccessful at times, is not morally narrow.

I

The use of "sense" and "sensibility" characters as foils to one another was a common practice with the novelists of Jane Austen's day.[4] In Frances Brooke's *Lady Julia Mandeville* (1763), for example, the prosperous love affair of the prudent, worldly-wise Lady Anne Wilmot was used to set off the tragic story of the languishing Lady Julia and her lover. In *A Simple Story* (1791) Elizabeth Inchbald contrasted her passionate and sensitive Miss Milner with the decorous, coldhearted Miss Fenton. Readers were sensitive

[3] Andrew Wright (*Jane Austen's Novels*, pp. 86–92) challenges the idea that Elinor is an image of static perfection on other grounds. He does not find positive flaws in her behavior or moral vision, but he holds that she "becomes increasingly sensitive as the book progresses" just as Marianne becomes increasingly sensible. As evidence for his views he cites the collapses of Elinor's composure which Lucy Steele's announcement of her engagement to Edward Farrars, and the ultimate revelation that Lucy has married Robert Farrars, produce. See also Henrietta Ten Harmsel, *A Study in Fictional Conventions*, pp. 48–49.

[4] I have chosen stories in which female characters are contrasted to illustrate this point. Male "sense" and "sensibility" characters were, of course, also contrasted, and in Mary Brunton's *Self-Control* (1810) a daughter's self-possession is contrasted with her father's sickly sensibility.

to, and appreciated, such contrasting character studies. The *Edinburgh Review* was quick to note the contrast between Rosamund Percy (sensibility) and her sister Caroline (sense) in Maria Edgeworth's *Patronage* (1814) and called the girls' characters "beautifully diversified":

> The keen but repressed feeling and subdued tenderness of the former [Caroline] are well contrasted by the quick and energetic qualities of the latter; and Rosamund's unenvious admiration of, and entire devotion to her sister, forms a most pleasing and affecting picture.[5]

Stories about "sense" and "sensibility" characters in which the importance of "sense" is emphasized would seem to have the most direct bearing on a discussion of Jane Austen's novel. Three such stories, all of which resemble *Sense and Sensibility* somewhat, are Maria Edgeworth's "Mademoiselle Panache,"[6] part 1, and Jane West's *A Gossip's Story* (1796) and *The Advantages of Education* (1793).[7] It will be necessary to summarize these stories in some detail in order to call attention to features pertinent to this discussion. In "Mademoiselle Panache" two sisters,

[5] *Edinburgh Review*, 13 (1813–1814): 420.

[6] The first part of "Mademoiselle Panache" appeared in Maria Edgeworth's *The Parent's Assistant* in 1795. The second half appeared in 1801 in her *Moral Tales*. In a letter to Anna Austen dated September 28, 1814, Jane Austen declares, "I have made up my mind to like no novels really, but Miss Edgeworth's, Yours and my own" (*Letters*, p. 405). She also mentions Miss Edgeworth in a letter of February 9, 1813 (*Letters*, p. 305), refers to her *Patronage* in a letter of August, 1814 (*Letters*, p. 398), and alludes to *Belinda* in *Northanger Abbey* (p. 40).

[7] Jane Austen mentions Mrs. West, in a manner that suggests a degree of familiarity with her works, in a letter of September 8, 1816 (*Letters*, p. 466). She mentions Mrs. West's *Alicia de Lacy* in a letter of September 28, 1814, saying, "I am quite determined . . . not to be pleased with Mrs. West's Alicia de Lacy, should I ever meet with it" (*Letters*, pp. 404–405).

Helen and Emma Temple, are contrasted. Emma is the sensible sister. "Helen, of a more vivacious temper, had not yet acquired her sister's good sense" the reader is told early in the story. She is a generous, well-meaning girl, but her impetuosity often gets her into difficulties. Contrary to Miss Edgeworth's intentions, the reader is inclined to find Helen a more attractive character than the rather priggish sister whose righteous rationality is continually opposed to Helen's blundering benevolence.

The first part of "Mademoiselle Panache" deals with experiences that teach Helen to be cautious in placing her affections and to be guided by reason and not by her emotions in judging other people. The Temple family make a new acquaintance, Lady Augusta ———. Lady Augusta is about the same age as the Temple sisters. She is pretty, vivacious, and apparently amiable; in fact, however, she is a coldhearted and unprincipled girl. The sensible Emma is polite but reserved during the first stages of her acquaintance with Lady Augusta, and, cautious judge of character that she is, soon begins to suspect that the girl is not what she seems to be. But the affectionate Helen is devoted to Lady Augusta almost from her "first impression" of the young lady. In a conversation which is reminiscent of Elinor Dashwood's argument with her mother after Willoughby's departure from Barton Cottage, Mrs. Temple wisely warns her daughter of the necessity for judging her new acquaintance rationally and with deliberation. "'Surely, mother,'" Helen says,

> "it would be but good-natured to believe a stranger to be amiable and sensible when we know nothing to the contrary . . . it would be very hard upon them, and very silly in us too, if we were to take it for granted they were everything that was bad, merely because they were strangers."

"You do not yet reason with perfect accuracy, Helen: is there no difference between thinking people everything that is good and amiable, and taking it for granted that they are everything that is bad?"

"But then, mother, what can one do?—To be always doubting and doubting is very disagreeable: and at first, when one knows nothing of a person, how can we judge?"

"There is no necessity, that I can perceive, for your judging of people's characters the very instant they come into a room. . . . And though it be disagreeable to be always 'doubting and doubting,' yet it is what we must submit to patiently, Helen, unless we would submit to the consequences of deciding ill; which, let me assure you, my little daughter, are infinitely more disagreeable."[8]

Mrs. Dashwood, it will be remembered, uses some arguments similar to Helen's, when she declares that Elinor would "'rather take evil upon credit than good'" in judging Willoughby. Mrs. Dashwood has explained Willoughby's departure to herself "'in the most satisfactory way'" by assuming that Mrs. Smith suspects his regard for Marianne and has banished him.

". . . but you, Elinor, who love to doubt where you can—It will not satisfy *you*, I know. . . . You will tell me, I know, that this may, or may *not* have happened; but I will listen to no cavil, unless you can point out any other method of understanding the affair as satisfactory as this. And now, Elinor, what have you to say?"

"Nothing, for you have anticipated my answer."

"Then you would have told me, that it might or might not have happened. Oh! Elinor, how incomprehensible are

[8] Maria Edgeworth, *The Parent's Assistant* (Philadelphia, 1854): "Mademoiselle Panache" (Part 1), pp. 318-319.

your feelings! You had rather take evil upon credit than good. You had rather look out for misery for Marianne and guilt for poor Willoughby, than an apology for the latter." (p. 78)

Mrs. Temple's warnings are no more efficacious than Elinor's are: without pausing to study the girl's character carefully, Helen becomes more and more attached to Lady Augusta. And like Willoughby, Lady Augusta proves to be unworthy of a heroine's affections. To her grief, Helen begins to learn the truth when she sees Lady Augusta deliberately disobey, and then deceive, her mother. Her eyes are fully opened when at a neighborhood ball Lady Augusta, who is now surrounded by a crowd of more fashionable acquaintances, snubs her. Thus Helen learns the need for caution and reserve. Lady Augusta pays for her sins in the latter part of "Mademoiselle Panache," a work discussed later in this study, when she elopes with a scoundrel named Dashwood.

In *A Gossip's Story* Jane West contrasts two sisters named Marianne and Louisa Dudley. The story of Marianne is a sermon on the dangers of an excess of sensibility and at times a parody, reminiscent in some ways of Jane Austen's "Love and Freindship," of the conventions of the romantic novel. Louisa Dudley illustrates the value of "sense." Mrs. West manages the praise of sense and condemnation of excessive sensibility more successfully than Maria Edgeworth does, in that her "sensibility" character does not run away with the reader's sympathies. Marianne Dudley's is a languishing, querulous, unhealthy sensibility; she lacks the charm and vitality of a Marianne Dashwood, the engaging impulsiveness of a Helen Temple. But Louisa Dudley is too good to be true. She is a sort of walking conduct book, whom one can neither believe in nor care about.[9] Toward the end of the novel, especially, her perfection is dwelt upon to such an extent that one is reminded of the parade of instances of the heroine's good judgment that makes the conclusion of *Pamela* so tedious.

Mrs. West's heroines were separated when their mother died. Marianne was brought up by a doting grandmother, and as Mrs. West relates, "though the gentle timidity of her temper had preserved her from the usual effects of early indulgence, it rendered her peculiarly unfit to encounter even those common calamities humanity must endure."[10] Moreover, Marianne "had long been an attentive reader of memoirs and adventures, and had transplanted into her gentle bosom all the soft feelings and highly refined sensibilities of the respective heroines" (vol. 1, chap. 4, p. 39). The result of her bad upbringing is that she has

> an amiable and ingenuous mind, solicitous to excel, and desirous to be happy, but destitute of natural vigour or acquired stability; forming to itself a romantick standard, to which nothing human ever attained; perplexed by imaginary difficulties; sinking under fancied evils; destroying its own peace by the very means which it takes to secure it; and acting with a degree of folly beneath the common level, through its desire of aspiring above the usual limits of female excellence. (vol. 1, chap. 5, p. 47)

From her grandmother Marianne has inherited a large fortune. Louisa Dudley has been brought up by her father,

[9] Compare the opinion of J. M. S. Tompkins in her "'Elinor and Marianne': A Note on Jane Austen," *The Review of English Studies*, 16 (1940): 33–43.

[10] Jane West, *A Gossip's Story and a Legendary Tale* (London, 1799), vol. 1, chap. 2, p. 19. All references will be to this edition.

and because of his tuition and example she is a model of prudence and self-control. She has a "well-regulated mind" and her manners are "placidly reserved" (vol. 1, chap. 2, p. 18). When the story begins, the family has been reunited. Although Mr. Dudley has suffered financial reverses, he has managed to secure a comfortable house in the country for his daughters.

Marianne is courted by a handsome, wealthy, and virtuous young man, Mr. Pelham. The affair, in her eyes, assumes the dimensions of an episode in a romantic novel. First Marianne decides, for no reason, that one of her friends is in love with Mr. Pelham. Heroically, she resolves "to sacrifice love . . . on the altar of friendship" (vol. 1, chap. 4, p. 39). This pleasure, however, is denied her. Further parody of the romantic novel is provided when Marianne concludes that if she and Pelham had been destined for one another the fact would have been manifest in a striking soul-similarity obvious from their first encounter. The mysterious instantaneous *rapport* of lovers in fiction being lacking, she can only conclude that "their sentiments did not coincide, their tastes were materially different, there was no similitude of soul, nothing to form that strong tie of sympathy which . . . must exist, or else there can be no certain expectation of felicity" (vol. 1, chap. 10, pp. 92–93). She resolves, however, to immolate herself on the altar of filial duty and marry Mr. Pelham. When Mr. Dudley assures her that he does not wish her to marry a man she cannot love, she decides that she will remain single all her life and share her fortune with her impoverished family. Louisa meanwhile is addressed by Sir William Milton. Knowing that her father is anxious to see her well settled, since she now has no expectations from him and no fortune of her own, she resolves to consider Sir William's suit, though she is secretly in love with Mr. Pelham. When the Dudleys learn that Sir William has seduced and deserted another young girl, he is dismissed.

Marianne is rescued from a runaway horse by a new neighbor, Mr. Clermont. In addition to introducing himself under circumstances gratifying to a reader of romantic novels, Clermont proves to be admirably suited to the temperament and tastes of a woman of feeling. He and Marianne soon discover that they are kindred souls:

> Never was such a wonderful coincidence of opinion! Both were passionate admirers of the country; both loved moonlight walks, and the noise of distant waterfalls; both were enchanted by the sound of the sweet-toned harp, and the almost equally soft cadence of the pastoral and elegiack muse; in short, whatever was passionate, elegant, and sentimental in art; or beautiful, pensive, and enchanting in nature. (vol. 1, chap. 16, p. 105) [11]

Unlike Jane Austen's Willoughby, Clermont does not prove to be a rake. He and Marianne are married. But their expectations of what marriage will prove to be are so high, and their sensitivity is so acute, that they make one another miserable, and their marriage ends in a *de facto* separation. Mr. Dudley dies, and Mr. Pelham is so struck by the Christian resignation that Louisa displays during her father's fatal illness that he falls in love with her. They are married, and the novel closes with lengthy descriptions of their marital bliss.

In her "'Elinor and Marianne': A Note on Jane Austen," J. M. S. Tompkins has suggested that *Sense and Sensibility*

[11] Note the similarity between this passage and *Sense and Sensibility*, p. 47.

is, to a large extent, a rewriting of *A Gossip's Story*.[12] Jane Austen, according to Miss Tomkins, simplified Mrs. West's plot, rejecting

> romantic and emotional plot-elements, which disturb the rhythm of daily life that Miss Austen seeks to establish. Elinor's self-command, like Louisa's, is tried by her love for an unresponsive man, but this man is not her sister's suitor. With the disappearance of this complication goes the now unnecessary Sir William Milton, but the discovery that had discredited him with the Dudleys, that he had seduced a girl and then abandoned her, serves for Colonel Brandon's story and discredits Willoughby. The heroine's loss of fortune and retirement into the country are retained in a much milder form and placed at the beginning of the book, while Marianne's heritage is abolished in order that her character and her sister's may develop under the same conditions. The deathbed beside which Louisa shines is replaced by the sick-bed of Marianne (an admirably economical stroke) and the colourless father by a mother young, foolish, and kind enough to leave her daughters to their own discretion.[13]

Since "Marianne's remorse was to be restorative, not hopeless,"[14] Miss Tompkins says, there is ultimate happiness, instead of an unsuccessful marriage, in store for her.

Sense and Sensibility appears to have affinities with so many works in addition to *A Gossip's Story* that I am not inclined to rate the influence of Mrs. West's novel on Jane

---

[12] See above note 9. In "An Unknown Source for *Sense and Sensibility*," *Studia Neophilologica*, 22 (1950): 146–170, Martin Melander also presents a case for *A Gossip's Story* as a source for *Sense and Sensibility*.

[13] Tompkins, "'Elinor and Marianne,'" p. 40.

[14] *Ibid.*, p. 42.

Austen as highly as Miss Tompkins does. As critics—among them Miss Tompkins—have pointed out, Jane Austen employs in *Sense and Sensibility* a number of characters who seem to derive from Fanny Burney and Samuel Richardson.[15] Again, Charlotte Smith's *Ethelinde* (1789) would seem to have had some influence on *Sense and Sensibility*. Her treatment of the brother of Ethelinde, who is notable for an absorption in himself that makes him unaware of the needs and wishes of his family, may to some extent have influenced Jane Austen's treatment of John Dashwood. Almost certainly a scene in which Ethelinde's brother decides that his impoverished father and sister do not need his assistance suggested the conversation in which Fanny and John Dashwood rationalize their failure to provide for Mrs. Dashwood and her daughters.[16] Moreover,

[15] See *ibid.*, p. 43; Alan D. McKillop's "The Context of *Sense and Sensibility*," *Rice Institute Pamphlets*, 44 (1957–1958): 65–77; the relevant chapter in Henrietta Ten Harmsel's *A Study in Fictional Conventions*; and E. E. Duncan-Jones's "The Misses Selby and Steele," *Times Literary Supplement*, September 10, 1964. I do not, obviously, concur with R. Brimley Johnson's opinion that Fanny Burney's *Camilla* was the source for *Sense and Sensibility*. (See R. Brimley Johnson's *Jane Austen* [London: Sheed & Ward, 1927], pp. 118–121, and 153; and his *Jane Austen: Her Life, Her Work, Her Family, and Her Critics* [London: J. M. Dent & Sons, 1930], pp. 133–134.) Miss Tompkins has argued fairly conclusively against Johnson's theory, on the grounds of what is known about the composition of *Sense and Sensibility*, in her "'Elinor and Marianne,'" p. 42. Moreover, although, as Johnson points out, there is a "sense-sensibility" opposition of a sort between Edgar Mandlebert and Camilla, such oppositions, as noted earlier, were by no means uncommon in the novels of Jane Austen's day; and the plot of *Sense and Sensibility* is much less similar to that of *Camilla* than it is to several other "sense and sensibility" novels.

[16] Charlotte Smith, *Ethelinde* (London, 1790), vol. 5, chap. 8, pp. 173–174. *Ethelinde* is alluded to in *Volume The Third* (*Minor Works*, p. 199). Alan D. McKillop notes the similarity between this passage and

one of the most important themes of *Sense and Sensibility*, the idea that impulsive young people are likely to be "deceived in Freindship and Betrayed in Love" by unworthy objects, and must learn to be cautious in placing their affections, is not stressed in *A Gossip's Story*. Marianne Dudley's Clermont, unlike Helen Temple's Lady Augusta —————— or Marianne Dashwood's Willoughby, is a genuinely good character; he falls out with Marianne because neither of them is mature enough for marriage. Jane Austen might have been impressed with Maria Edgeworth's treatment of the theme of misplaced affections. Again, she and her readers might have encountered the theme in another "sense and sensibility" novel by Mrs. West, the novel entitled *The Advantages of Education*.

In *The Advantages of Education* Maria Williams is a young girl of strong sensibility and not overmuch judgment. Like Marianne Dashwood, and unlike Marianne Dudley, Maria is a vivacious and engaging young lady. The role of "sense" character is played by Maria's mother, whose prudence and good judgment stand the daughter in good stead. To the impetuous and affectionate Maria this "calm monitress" advocates the same kind of caution that Elinor Dashwood and Maria Edgeworth's Mrs. Temple recommend: "'While artifice and deceit are so prevalent in the world,'" Mrs. Williams tells her daughter,

> "we ought (even before we form an intimate connexion with any one) to examine every action, and to applaud no virtue, of whose existence we are doubtful. As this cautious

---

Sense and Sensibility, pp. 8–13, in his "Allusions to Prose Fiction in Jane Austen's *Volume the Third*," *Notes and Queries*, 196 (1951): 428–429.

conduct is totally incompatible with quick decisions, we should ever beware of forming hasty conclusions, and habituate our minds to suspect a spontaneous plaudit."[17]

The worth of Mrs. Williams' advice is demonstrated in the course of an unfortunate love affair, much more nearly similar to Marianne Dashwood's than Marianne Dudley's is, between Maria Williams and an attractive young rake named Sir Henry Neville. Jane Austen need not, as Miss Tompkins has suggested, have combined the passion and charm of Clermont and the libertinism of Sir William Milton to produce Willoughby; these qualities were already combined in the character of Sir Henry. The tenderhearted Maria believes the handsome young man's professions of love, little suspecting that he is a young Lovelace who hopes to persuade her to run away with him. Mrs. Williams, however, notices that Sir Henry seems unwilling to give any information about himself or his connections, and is suspicious of him. It is revealed that Sir Henry has seduced and deserted another young girl, and Maria gives him up. When the young lady whom he has seduced dies, Sir Henry commits suicide. Like Marianne Dashwood, Maria has another suitor, less attractive but more virtuous than her first love, whom she comes to love after she rejects Sir Henry. *The Advantages of Education* also contains some parody of favorite themes and situations in the novel of sensibility. In particular, it satirizes the "sensibility" heroine's tendency to go into a "decline" as a result of frustrated love, a point to be discussed later.

It would seem, then, that *Sense and Sensibility* ought not

[17] Jane West, *The Advantages of Education* (London, 1793), vol. 2, chap. 1, p. 11.

to be considered as a rewriting of any particular source.[18] One may, however, take the three works just discussed as typical of the criticism of sensibility with which Jane Austen was familiar and as works likely to have influenced her; and it will be worthwhile to make some comparisons between them and *Sense and Sensibility*.

II

Sense and Sensibility is the product of reworkings of the prototype "Elinor and Marianne" which was composed long before the version known today was published. There is every reason to believe that in one or more of its early forms the novel was very close to typical criticisms of sensibility such as Maria Edgeworth's or Mrs. West's. Even in the story as it stands Elinor and Marianne Dashwood are easily recognizable as refined versions of the standard "sense" and "sensibility" characters of the satirists. Their careers follow patterns similar to those established by the critics of sensibility: Marianne's errors in judgment, the hastily formed attachment, the revelation of the unworthiness of the romantically attractive Willoughby, Marianne's reformation, her marriage to a worthy but unglamorous man, Elinor's response to the tribulations of her love affair, her ultimate reward—all of these things are paralleled in other works of the period. And there are numerous local hints of a rather broad parody of the stock materials of the novel of sensibility that are reminiscent of Mrs. West or, for that matter, Jane Austen's own attacks on the novel of

[18] I have discussed the problem of *A Gossip's Story* as the "source" for *Sense and Sensibility* more explicitly in my "*Sense and Sensibility* and Its Sources," in *The Review of English Studies*, 17 (1966): 413–419.

sensibility in "Love and Freindship." Ian Watt cites Marianne's speeches on poetry and picturesque landscape as indications of her origin in parody, and adds that "Jane Austen is obviously parodying the sentimental heroine's stock reactions to places that remind her of lost love" when she refers to Marianne's "moments of precious, of invaluable misery" at Cleveland, the Palmer family's seat.[19] A more glaring example of such "stock reactions" is Marianne's "dear Norland" speech:

> "Dear, dear Norland!... when shall I cease to regret you!—when learn to feel a home elsewhere!—Oh! happy house, could you know what I suffer in now viewing you from this spot, from whence perhaps I may view you no more!—And you too, ye well-known trees!—but you will continue the same.—No leaf will decay because we are removed, nor any branch become motionless although we can observe you no longer!—No; you will continue the same; unconscious of the pleasure or the regret you occasion, and insensible of any change in those who walk under your shade!—But who will remain to enjoy you?" (p. 27)

Flowery addresses to beloved spots were part of the stock in trade of the heroine of sensibility,[20] and Marianne's sentiments and rhetoric are suspiciously reminiscent of, for example, the first words we hear from Amanda Fitzallen,

[19] In the introduction to *Sense and Sensibility*, ed. Ian Watt (New York: Harper & Row, 1961). The essay has been reproduced in Watt's *Jane Austen: A Collection of Critical Essays* (Englewood Cliffs, New Jersey: Prentice-Hall, 1963), pp. 45–51, and it is to p. 45 of the essay in Watt's anthology that the citations above refer.

[20] B. C. Southam, *Jane Austen's Literary Manuscripts* (London: Oxford University Press, 1964), p. 56, makes this point.

the heroine of Regina Maria Roche's *The Children of the Abbey* (1798):

> "Hail, sweet asylum of my infancy! Content and innocence reside beneath your humble roof, and charity unboastful of the good it renders. Hail, ye venerable trees! my happiest hours of childish gaity were passed beneath your shelter— then, careless as the birds that sung upon your boughs, I laughed the hours away, nor knew of evil."[21]

Characters in Mrs. Radcliffe's works often make similar speeches. There are hints of parody similar to Mrs. West's when Jane Austen has her Marianne also speak of that mysterious sympathy of souls, accompanied by a striking similarity in tastes, which, according to the novel of sensibility, was the only basis for true love and friendship. "'I could not be happy with a man whose taste did not in every point coincide with my own,'" Marianne declares. "'He must enter into all my feelings; the same books, the same music must charm us both'" (p. 17). Again, the report of her first conversation with Willoughby ridicules romantic affinity of soul in much the same manner as *A Gossip's Story* does:

> Their taste was strikingly alike. The same books, the same passages were idolized by each—or if any difference appeared, any objection arose, it lasted no longer than till the force of her arguments and the brightness of her eyes could be displayed. He acquiesced in all her decisions, caught all her enthusiasm; and long before his visit concluded, they conversed with the familiarity of a long-established acquaintance. (p. 47)

[21] Regina Maria Roche, *The Children of the Abbey* (Philadelphia, 1860), vol. I, chap. I, p. I. But of course Jane Austen could not have read it before beginning *Sense and Sensibility*.

And the fact that Marianne's and Willoughby's acquaintance, like that of Marianne Dudley and Clermont, begins with a romantic rescue also smacks of parody.

On the other hand it is equally clear that an aesthetic gulf of considerable magnitude separates *Sense and Sensibility* from its analogues, probably as the result of the revisions to which the original "Elinor and Marianne" was subjected. Marianne and Elinor Dashwood are credible human beings rather than mere quasi-allegorical stock figures. Marianne is less exclusively a parody of the sentimental heroine than Marianne Dudley, less of a "humors" character than Maria Edgeworth's Helen Temple. Her bias toward sensibility is modified by a good critical intelligence, and she is less incredibly naïve than the heroines of Jane West and Maria Edgeworth. In addition to her sense, the reader is told, Elinor Dashwood "had an excellent heart; her disposition was affectionate, and her feelings were strong" (p. 6). And there is some evidence in the novel—although one might wish for more—to support this statement: her convincingly portrayed breakdowns after reading Willoughby's dismissal of Marianne and after learning the truth about Lucy Steele's marriage are enough to separate her from Mrs. West's Louisa Dudley, who remains composed even at her father's deathbed.

But I am concerned here with another sort of difference between *Sense and Sensibility* and its analogues. Jane Austen not only refines and modifies her borrowed character types but also at times ironically reverses the attitude of the typical fictional criticism of sensibility toward the stock figures of the "sensible sister" and her foil, and uses this ironic reversal to help define her own more complex moral vision. I believe, too, that she relies on her early nineteenth-century reader's familiarity with the convention within which she is working to make her departures apparent to him. If *Sense and Sensibility* is considered in terms of its relationship to other criticisms of sensibility it becomes clear that two things in Jane Austen's story—Elinor Dashwood's attitude toward the grief-induced illness from which Marianne almost dies toward the end of the novel, and her reaction to Willoughby's disgraceful conduct—are cleverly designed to help undermine the moral position of her "sensible sister," to convict Elinor of a failure in "emotional intelligence" comparable to Marianne's failures in moral-emotional perception.

In chapter 7 of the third volume of *Sense and Sensibility* the reader is repeatedly informed that, while Colonel Brandon and Mrs. Jennings fear the worst effects from the cold that Marianne has caught as a result of her melancholy rambles through the grounds of Mr. Palmer's estate, Elinor refuses to believe that it will develop into anything serious. During the early stages of Marianne's illness, Colonel Brandon is "astonished at her sister's composure, who, though attending and nursing her the whole day, against Marianne's inclination, and forcing proper medicines on her at night, trusted, like Marianne, to the certainty and efficacy of sleep, and felt no real alarm" (p. 307). When the apothecary pronounced Marianne's illness "to have a putrid tendency," Mrs. Jennings, "who had been inclined from the first to think Marianne's complaint more serious than Elinor, now looked very grave" (p. 307). But Elinor, supported by the apothecary, refuses to be alarmed. Two days later, Jane Austen says, the apothecary "still talked boldly of a speedy recovery, and Miss Dashwood was equally sanguine;"

but the expectation of the others was by no means so cheerful. Mrs. Jennings had determined very early in the seisure that Marianne would never get over it, and Colonel Brandon, who was chiefly of use in listening to Mrs. Jennings's forebodings, was not in a state of mind to resist their influence. (p. 309)

At first it appears that the sensible Elinor is about to triumph again:

On the morning of the third day ... the gloomy anticipations of [Colonel Brandon and Mrs. Jennings] were almost done away; for when Mr. Harriss arrived, he declared his patient materially better. ... Elinor, confirmed in every pleasant hope, was all cheerfulness; rejoicing that in her letters to her mother, she had pursued her own judgment rather than her friend's, in making very light of the indisposition which delayed them at Cleveland; and almost fixing on the time when Marianne would be able to travel. (p. 310)

But within a few hours the fears of Colonel Brandon and Mrs. Jennings are justified. Marianne is in a very serious state, and Elinor is "reproaching herself with having trifled with so many days of illness, and wretched for some immediate relief" (p. 312). Why is it that Elinor's minimizing of her sister's illness and her subsequent remorse when Marianne proves to be in real danger are so emphatically stressed?

Mrs. Jennings and Colonel Brandon are predicting for Marianne what in the parlance of the romantic novelists of Jane Austen's day would be called a "decline," brought on by emotional stress. When her prognosis has been confirmed by Marianne's turn for the worse, Mrs. Jennings does not scruple "to attribute the severity and danger of the attack to the many weeks of previous indisposition which Marianne's disappointment had brought on" (p. 314). In Elinor's opinion, however, women—even women such as Marianne —do not die of love. Marianne has a cold, the apothecary has pronounced her to be in no danger, and Elinor is not going to "make a fuss" about the illness and send to Barton for her mother.

The significance of the incident, and of Elinor's remorse, become clearer when one remembers that the decline was a favorite target for parody to critics of the novel of sensibility—Jane Austen among them. Mrs. West, as noted earlier, ridiculed the decline in *The Advantages of Education.* In that work Maria Williams' best friend, who is more romantic, and much sillier, than Maria herself, acts as a go-between for Maria and Sir Henry Neville. When the lovers are separated for a brief period, Maria becomes ill. Her friend is sure that Maria is dying of love and loneliness, and sends for Sir Henry immediately—only to learn that Maria's illness is nothing more dramatic than a case of measles. Jane Austen herself had parodied the decline in "Love and Freindship." There the unfortunate Sophia, who is expiring in a "galloping Consumption" as a result of the series of fainting fits that she has enjoyed upon hearing of her beloved Augustus' death, delivers this parting speech:

> "My beloved Laura . . . take warning from my unhappy End and avoid the imprudent conduct which had occasioned it. . . . Beware of fainting-fits. . . . Though at the time they may be refreshing and agreeable yet believe me they will in the end, if too often repeated and at improper seasons, prove destructive to your Constitution. . . . My fate will teach you this. . . . I die a Martyr to my greif for the loss of Augustus. . . . One fatal swoon has cost me my

Life. . . . Beware of swoons Dear Laura. . . . A frenzy fit is not one quarter so pernicious; it is an exercise to the Body and if not too violent, is I dare say conducive to Health in its consequences—Run mad as often as you chuse; but do not faint—." (*Minor Works*, p. 102)

In fact, considering that *Sense and Sensibility* seems originally to have been a rather thorough parody of the career of a heroine of sensibility, is it not likely that Marianne's illness itself may have been a satire on the decline at some stage in the development of the novel? I suspect that the illness originally ended in an anticlimax, just as Maria Williams' mock decline does, and that Jane Austen later revised the incident. Such a theory would account for a rather strange phenomenon in *Sense and Sensibility*: the inappropriately humorous tone of Jane Austen's early references to Marianne's illness and Colonel Brandon's and Mrs. Jennings' reactions to it. Colonel Brandon's fears are at first presented as the rather amusing oversolicitude of a man in love, and Mrs. Jennings' determination that Marianne's broken heart will be the death of her provokes a smile at her sentimentality. In passages such as the one in which Jane Austen writes that "Mrs. Jennings had determined very early in the seisure that Marianne would never get over it, and Colonel Brandon, who was chiefly of use in listening to Mrs. Jennings's forebodings, was not in a state of mind to resist their influence," for instance, her tone seems to jar somewhat, in view of what the outcome of the seizure is to be. Is this not an indication that Jane Austen originally treated Marianne's illness differently, and that in altering the episode she did not quite succeed in effacing all the traces of the way in which it was originally handled? Speculations about the novel's prototypes aside, however, the incident in *Sense and Sensibility* as we have it seems to have considerable significance. Jane Austen and her audience were prepared to expect that in a criticism of the heroine of sensibility such as hers, the logical thing to have happen is that a "decline" will turn out anticlimactically, that Elinor's sensible attitude toward her sister's illness will be justified. And when what actually happens is that the incident turns out seriously, the fact throws into strong relief a significant difference between *Sense and Sensibility* and more ordinary criticisms of sensibility.

For in *Sense and Sensibility* the incident is not a criticism of sensibility but a criticism of "sense" and of Elinor Dashwood. It is only Elinor who belittles the possibility of dying of love; Jane Austen grants Marianne a genuine decline—giving it an air of probability by having Marianne catch a cold as a result of her grief-stricken wanderings in inclement weather, and having the cold take a serious turn because of her despondency and her already weakened state of health. What Jane Austen has done in this part of *Sense and Sensibility* is to forsake the attitude of the critic of sensibility herself, transfer it to Elinor, and then leave Elinor "holding the bag."

This is not the only time that Elinor has assumed the role of the satirist of sensibility; minimizing the importance of Marianne's grief-induced illness is only one manifestation of a general tendency on Elinor's part. Elinor's emotions are naturally less intense than Marianne's, and they are kept in check by her habits of self-control. Naturally enough, perhaps, since she has lived with Marianne's excesses, and her mother's indulgence of them, all her life, she tends to view her sister's emotionalism with an irony that at times comes close to being unpleasantly sharp. She is constantly cutting Marianne's grandiose romantic effusions down to size. Thus when she discusses Marianne's opinions on eternal constancy with Colonel Brandon she counters the tolerant older man's defense of the "'amiable ... prejudices of a young mind,'" and eagerly reduces her sister's romantic ideas to absurdity. "'Your sister, I understand,'" Colonel Brandon says,

"does not approve of second attachments."
"No," replied Elinor, "her opinions are all romantic."
"Or rather, as I believe, she considers them impossible to exist."
"I believe she does. But how she contrives it without reflecting on the character of her own father, who had himself two wives, I know not." (pp. 55–56)

And when Marianne defends love and a "competence" against the "riches" which Elinor considers useful to happiness, Elinor quickly and gleefully exposes the fact that her own notion of "riches" is more modest than Marianne's notion of "competence." "'What have wealth or grandeur to do with happiness?'" Marianne exclaims. "'Grandeur has but little,'" Elinor replies, "'but wealth has much to do with it.'"

"Elinor, for shame! ... money can only give happiness where there is nothing else to give it. Beyond a competence, it can afford no real satisfaction, as far as mere self is concerned."
"Perhaps ... we may come to the same point. *Your* competence and *my* wealth are very much alike, I dare say; and without them, as the world goes now, we shall both agree that every kind of external comfort must be wanting. Your ideas are only more noble than mine. Come, what is your competence?"

"About eighteen hundred or two thousand a-year; not more than *that*."
... "*Two* thousand a-year! *One* is my wealth! I guessed how it would end." (p. 91)

On numerous occasions throughout *Sense and Sensibility* Elinor enjoys exposing the follies of sensibility. And although she is not heartless enough to laugh at Marianne's extreme reaction to her disappointment in love, she does tend to remember that, after all, Marianne will get over it—perhaps sooner than Elinor herself will recover from her own unhappy affair. When Colonel Brandon inquires anxiously about Marianne's reactions to Willoughby's perfidy, Elinor replies, "'Her sufferings have been very severe. I have only to hope that they may be proportionably short'" (pp. 199–200). And she is quite aware that she herself has managed to bear up well under a similar disappointment.

But Elinor's attitude toward her sister's sensibility is proved to be unjust as far as the incident of Marianne's illness is concerned. With Marianne on the verge of death, Elinor is forced to admit that a decline brought on by frustrated love is more than a romantic illusion. She feels "all the reasonableness" of Mrs. Jennings' analysis of Marianne's state and the idea gives "fresh misery to her reflections" (p. 314). Behind the remorse and self-reproach with which Elinor is filled when her sister's illness turns out to be critical lies the feeling that her irony has been to some extent a manifestation of a lack of sympathy and understanding for a temperament different from her own. In *Persuasion* Jane Austen says that Captain Wentworth, faced with Mrs. Musgrove's belated and unattractive display of feeling for her son Richard, "shewed the kindest consideration for all that was real and unabsurd in the parent's feelings" (p. 68). Elinor Dashwood proves to have been too sensitive to what is absurd, and not sensitive enough to what is real, in her sister's sensibility. She, as well as Marianne, is given a moral eye-opening. And as Jane Austen's "sensible sister" is shocked into a degree of self-knowledge, her author defines her own moral vision in opposition to that of the too complacent critics—perhaps the Jane Austen of "Love and Freindship" and "Elinor and Marianne" is among them—of sensibility.

III

Jane Austen attacks another aspect of Elinor's "sense"— in a way that also reflects upon the too harsh critics of sensibility—in her treatment of Elinor's reactions to the sinful Willoughby. Elinor's "sense" consists not only in her ironic attitude toward Marianne's emotionalism but also in her caution regarding human relationships, her tendency to trust, as Maria Edgeworth's Emma Temple and Jane West's Mrs. Williams do, to facts and evidence rather than intuition and emotional responses in making judgments. Thus in the conversation that takes place after Willoughby's departure from the Dashwoods' neighborhood, as noted previously, Mrs. Dashwood, like Marianne, trusts in her affection for Willoughby. Elinor too is fond of him: "'I love Willoughby, sincerely love him,'" she declares (p. 81). But she reminds her mother of the bare facts of the situation: "'I confess ... that every circumstance except *one* is in favour of their engagement; but that *one* is the total silence of both on the subject, and with me it almost outweighs every other'" (p. 80). Willoughby has left without making a formal declaration of his intentions, and Elinor, in spite of her affection for him, is suspicious.

Elinor's caution is justified, where the complete trust of Marianne and her mother is not; but in one respect Elinor's rationality causes her to reach a less accurate estimate of Willoughby than Marianne and Mrs. Dashwood reach with their sensibility. Presented, later in the story, with further "facts" about Willoughby—the letter to Marianne and Colonel Brandon's story—Elinor is quick to decide that Willoughby is a callous libertine who has never cared for Marianne at all; seen through her eyes, he is another Sir Henry Neville. Elinor's opinion is not unjustified, one feels, for Colonel Brandon, unlike some of Jane Austen's other misleaders—Wickham and Frank Churchill, for instance— always seems to be a perfectly trustworthy interpreter of events. And the solution to the problem of Willoughby's letter—that the letter was written by his malevolent fiancée— is something the reader cannot blame Elinor or himself for failing to suspect. Nevertheless, unskillfully as she contrives it, Jane Austen shows that her rational and suspicious "sensible sister" has in some respects been a less accurate judge of Willoughby than Marianne has been. Even in the face of Colonel Brandon's "facts" Marianne has refused to judge Willoughby as harshly as her sister does. She longs to "'be allowed to think that he was not *always* acting a part, not *always* deceiving me;—but above all, if I could be assured that he never was so *very* wicked as my fears have sometimes fancied him, since the story of that unfortunate girl—'" (p. 344). And it turns out that there is truth in her feelings about him. Willoughby, weak and selfish as he is, proves to be not quite what Elinor has thought him. He has loved and still loves Marianne, and although he has seduced

Colonel Brandon's ward he has not, as Elinor and Colonel Brandon imagine, deliberately abandoned her to misery. Elinor becomes aware of her failure to do complete justice to Willoughby during her interview with him at Cleveland. During the interview she admits to him: "'You have proved yourself, on the whole, less faulty than I had believed you. You have proved your heart less wicked, much less wicked'" (pp. 329–330). And, reflecting on his story, she sees him as "a man who, to every advantage of person and talents, united a disposition naturally open and honest, and a feeling, affectionate temper. The world had made him extravagant and vain—Extravagance and vanity had made him cold-hearted and selfish" (p. 331). "Willoughby," the reader is told, "'poor Willoughby,' as she now allowed herself to call him, was constantly in her thoughts; she would not but have heard his vindication for the world, and now blamed, now acquitted herself for having judged him so harshly before" (pp. 334–335). It turns out, ironically, that Mrs. Dashwood's accusation that Elinor would "rather take evil upon credit than good" is not altogether unjust. It is possible to be too sensible as well as too trusting in one's approach to human relations.[22]

Marianne Dashwood's illness may have been designed at one time to parody the "decline" of the heroine of sensibility. Similarly, in an early version of *Sense and Sensibility* may Willoughby not have been merely an attractive but evil seducer like Mrs. West's Sir Henry Neville, a character designed to teach a too-romantic young lady a lesson?

[22] Compare the opinion of Marvin Mudrick (*Irony as Defense and Discovery*, p. 85) on this scene. Mudrick takes the changed attitude toward Willoughby as an indication of the lack of heart behind Jane Austen's moralizing.

Probably Jane Austen, reconsidering, embodied in Elinor's feelings about Willoughby the critical novelist's treatment of such figures, and then, again leaving Elinor "holding the bag," had her proved partially wrong. This hypothesis would help to explain why the revelation that Willoughby is not such a thorough rake as he appears comes as rather a surprise to the reader: Colonel Brandon's charge that Willoughby is the traditional callous seducer and deserter of young girls originally *was* the whole truth; and at a later date Jane Austen added extenuating circumstances to the affair with Colonel Brandon's ward, made Willoughby genuinely love Marianne, and then failed to cover her traces with adequate preparation for Willoughby's partial vindication. At any rate, it is safe to assume that Jane Austen hoped that her readers would see something unusual in her treatment of her attractive rake, and realize that by granting him a pardon she is indicting her "sensible sister" for being a little too sensible.

Had Mrs. West, or Jane Austen in the mood of "Love and Freindship"—perhaps in the mood of "Elinor and Marianne"—produced *Sense and Sensibility*, Marianne Dashwood's illness would have been a parody of the "decline" of the heroine of sensibility and Willoughby would have been merely a callous seducer introduced to demonstrate Marianne's folly. But Jane Austen has used Willoughby and Marianne's illness to undermine the traditional position of the "sensible sister" in criticisms of sensibility, and thus to define and emphasize her own moral vision. Understanding the relationship of Jane Austen's novel to other similar works of the period helps one to appreciate more fully what Jane Austen is trying to say. Particularly it helps the reader to see that Elinor Dashwood is not the novel's standard of moral perfection but one of its candidates for self-knowledge, and to perceive that *Sense and Sensibility* is intended to be not merely an encomium of "sense" but a demonstration that both "sense" and "sensibility" have their limitations.

3

Pride and Prejudice and the "Patrician Hero"

In *Pride and Prejudice*, it is generally agreed, one encounters a variant of the eighteenth-century "art-nature" contrast when Elizabeth Bennet's forceful and engaging individualism clashes with Darcy's by no means indefensible respect for the social order and his class pride. Most critics agree that *Pride and Prejudice* does not suffer from the appearance of one-sidedness that makes *Sense and Sensibility* unattractive. It is obvious that neither Elizabeth nor Darcy embodies the moral norm of the novel. Each is admirable in his way, and each must have his pride and prejudice corrected by self-knowledge and come to a fuller appreciation of the other's temperament and beliefs. Ultimately their conflicting points of view are adjusted, and each achieves a mean between "nature" and "art." Elizabeth gains some appreciation of Darcy's sound qualities and comes to see the validity of class relationships. Darcy, under Elizabeth's influence, gains in naturalness and learns to respect the innate dignity of the individual.[1]

[1] The most detailed study of *Pride and Prejudice* in terms of the "art-nature" dichotomy is Samuel Kliger's "Jane Austen's *Pride and Prejudice* in the Eighteenth-Century Mode," *University of Toronto*

This essay is concerned with the relationship between certain elements in *Pride and Prejudice* and the novels of Richardson, Fanny Burney, and some of their imitators. Jane Austen's Mr. Darcy bears a marked resemblance to what may be called the "patrician hero," a popular character type in the novels of her day, and it is rewarding to investigate the relationship between Darcy and his love affair with Elizabeth Bennet and the heroes of Richardson's and Burney's novels and their relations with their heroines. Jane Austen's treatment of her patrician hero has a marked relevance to the theme of the reconciliation of opposite values and qualities that plays such an important part in *Pride and Prejudice*. Moreover, it is possible that the study of Darcy's origins may help to account for some inconsistencies in his character that have troubled a number of Jane Austen's readers. I shall begin by outlining some of the characteristics of the patrician hero.

I

Authority figures of various sorts play prominent roles in many eighteenth- and nineteenth-century novels. There is the patriarch or matriarch—Fielding's benevolent Allworthy, Godwin's terrifying Falkland, Dickens' Miss Havisham—whose relationship with a young dependent

---

Quarterly, 16 (1947): 357–370. To note only a few more instances of similar interpretations, Dorothy Van Ghent, in *The English Novel*, p. 100, states that the novel deals with "the difficult and delicate reconciliation of the sensitively developed individual with the terms of his social existence"; and David Daiches, in the introduction to the Modern Library edition of *Pride and Prejudice* (New York: Random House, 1950), calls the conflict between Elizabeth and Darcy an "adjustment between the claims of personal and social life."

acts as a sort of metaphor for the relationship between the social order and individual, "natural" man. In the novels of Richardson the relationship—prosperous, or, in the case of Lovelace and Clarissa, mutually destructive—between a young man of rank and fortune and a girl who is naturally good but socially inferior performs a similar function. The chief concern here is with the particular sort of figure that Richardson's Sir Charles Grandison represents.[2]

Richardson's Lovelace is a lost soul; his Mr. B—— has to be reformed by the virtuous Pamela. In Sir Charles Grandison, however, Richardson depicted a perfect Christian aristocrat. Sir Charles, Richardson would have his readers feel, combines the glamor of a Lovelace with the principles of a Clarissa. He is handsome and accomplished, dresses exquisitely (out of respect for his father's memory!) and has charming manners. He is immensely wealthy, an owner of splendid mansions and manors, and a powerful, important landholder. Yet he is a man of the strictest Christian virtue, a just, benevolent, and superefficient steward of his estates, a protector of the weak and a friend to the poor. In short, as Richardson describes him in the

---

[2] Jane Austen's Mr. Darcy is sometimes compared to Richardson's patrician "villain-hero," Mr. B——. E. E. Duncan-Jones, in "Proposals of Marriage in *Pamela* and *Pride and Prejudice*," *Notes and Queries*, 202 (1957): 76, has suggested that the proposal scene in *Pride and Prejudice* is a reminiscence of Mr. B——'s first honorable proposal to Pamela. More general resemblances in situation and character types between *Pamela* and Jane Austen's novel are discussed in Henrietta Ten Harmsel's "The Villain-Hero in *Pamela* and *Pride and Prejudice*," in *College English*, 23 (1961): 104–108, and in the chapter on *Pride and Prejudice* in Miss Ten Harmsel's *A Study in Fictional Conventions*. While it may be profitable to compare *Pamela* and *Pride and Prejudice*, it seems more rewarding to compare Darcy to heroes modeled on Sir Charles Grandison, for reasons to be made apparent later.

preface to *Grandison*, Sir Charles is "a man of religion and
virtue; of liveliness and spirit; accomplished and agreeable;
happy in himself, and a blessing to others." [3]

In the concluding note to *Grandison*, Richardson admits
that "it has been observed by some, that, in general [Sir
Charles] approaches too near the faultless character which
some critics censure as above nature" (7: 327). The reaction
Richardson describes is not uncommon among readers of
his novel. "Pictures of perfection," Jane Austen once
wrote, ". . . make me sick and wicked" (*Letters*, pp.
486–487, March 23, 1817); and most readers are wicked
enough to resent a character who demands so much admiration as Sir Charles does. In addition to being dismayed
by Sir Charles' incredible glamor and goodness, one tends
to be annoyed by the sycophantic deference with which he
is treated by nearly every character in his history. Sir Charles'
male friends attempt to emulate his virtues—and admit it
on every possible occasion. His female acquaintance worship
him as "the best of men," take his word for law, and all too
frequently fall in love with him. His admirers—repeatedly,
indeed *ad nauseam*—entrust their most important affairs
to him when they are living, and leave their estates to his
management when they die. Thus, Sir Charles, at his
sister's request, frees her from an unfortunate engagement;
later he arranges a suitable marriage for her. He extricates
his uncle from the clutches of an unmanageable mistress
and, on the uncle's insistence, provides him with a worthy
wife. He assists in bringing about a reconciliation between
his friend Mr. Beauchamp and Beauchamp's stepmother.

[3] *Sir Charles Grandison*, in *The Novels of Samuel Richardson*
(London: Chapman & Hall, 1902), 14: x. All references will be to this
edition.

He sees to it that the relatives of Mr. Danby—Mr. Danby having left his estate in Sir Charles' hands—are provided with fortunes, employment, and matrimonial partners, and arranges for the distribution of the remainder of Danby's estate in charity. He is entrusted with the negotiation of a "treaty" between the unfortunate Lady Clementina della Poretta and the tyrannical relatives from whom she flees to England. Indeed, it is a rare moment when Sir Charles is not dispensing advice and assistance to half a dozen of his family and friends simultaneously. "Such a man," the lovelorn Harriet Byron writes shortly after she has come to visit Sir Charles and Miss Grandison, "cannot, ought not to be engrossed by one family. . . . Let me enumerate some of his present engagements that we know of."

> The Danby family must have some further portion of his time.
>
> The executorship in the disposal of the 3000 £ in charity, in France as well as in England, will take up a good deal more.
>
> My Lord W—— may be said to be under his tutelage, as to the future happiness of his life.
>
> Miss Jervois's affairs, and the care he has for her person, engage much of his attention.
>
> He is his own steward. . . .
>
> His sister's match with Lord G—— is one of his cares.
>
> He has services to perform for his friend Beauchamp, with his father and mother-in-law, for the facilitating his coming over.
>
> And the Bologna family in its various branches, and more especially Signor Jeronymo's dangerous state of health, and Signora Clementina's disordered mind—O Lucy!—What leisure has this man to be in love! (vol. 4, letter 5, pp. 49–50)

Among the most fervent of Sir Charles' *aficionados* is the heroine of *Grandison*, Miss Byron. Sir Charles is her oracle; she treasures up his every word, and is embarrassingly grateful when he "condescends" to give her advice. She makes no pretensions to equality with her hero. She asks only that he: "'Teach me, sir, to be good, to be generous, to be forgiving—like you!—Bid me do what you think proper for me to do'" (vol. 6, letter 24, p. 206). Her relationship with him is like that of an adoring younger sister to an older brother, or that of an infatuated pupil with a favorite teacher: he is, to use her own word, her "monitor," as much as he is her lover. Harriet is in love with Sir Charles long before she knows that he cares for her; and when, after months of heartburning, she learns that he has decided to marry her, she is overwhelmed with joy and gratitude. "My single heart, methinks," she writes in her last letter to her grandmother,

> is not big enough to contain the gratitude which such a lot demands. Let the over-flowings of your pious joy, my dearest grandmamma, join with my thankfulness, in paying part of the immense debt for
>
> Your undeservedly happy
HARRIET GRANDISON.
(vol. 8, letter 62, p. 325)

As noted above, all of this deference, added to Richardson's insistence on Sir Charles' perfection, tends to make the reader react unfavorably toward both Sir Charles and his creator. One is inclined, in spite of Richardson's insistence on his humility, to think of Sir Charles as a stuffily superior, rather supercilious character, rather than as the noble and magnanimous hero that Richardson envisioned, and inclined, too, to tax Richardson as well as some of the characters in his novel with an unduly sycophantic attitude toward his highborn hero. That Jane Austen reacted to *Grandison* in a similar fashion will become apparent later.

All of the three novels that Fanny Burney published before 1813 deal, as *Sir Charles Grandison* does, with the relationships between exemplary young authority figures who are wealthy or wellborn or both and heroines who are in some respects their social inferiors. *Cecilia*, however, is the Burneyan novel most frequently cited as a source for *Pride and Prejudice*, some critics, indeed, feeling that Jane Austen's novel is simply a realistic rewriting of *Cecilia*. R. Brimley Johnson, for instance, has referred to the "title and plot, the leading characters and most dramatic scenes of *Pride and Prejudice*" as "frank appropriations" from *Cecilia*.[4]

Cecilia is certainly an important source for *Pride and Prejudice*. In plot and theme it resembles Jane Austen's novel more nearly than any other single work does. It is possible—though by no means certain—that the title of *Pride and Prejudice* was borrowed from *Cecilia*.[5] It is often

[4] The quotation is from Johnson's introduction to *Sense and Sensibility* in *The Works of Jane Austen* (London: J. M. Dent & Sons, 1950), p. v. The relationship between *Cecilia* and *Pride and Prejudice* is more fully discussed in Johnson's *Jane Austen*, pp. 124–127, and in his *Jane Austen: Her Life, Her Work, Her Family, and Her Critics*, pp. 137–139.

[5] *Cecilia* is not necessarily the source for the title of *Pride and Prejudice*, since the terms "pride" and "prejudice" were frequently used in conjunction in Jane Austen's day. R. W. Chapman's notes to the Oxford edition of *Pride and Prejudice* and numerous articles in the *Times Literary Supplement* and *Notes and Queries* testify to the popularity of the expression. I have myself located versions of the phrase within the Austen family circle, in the sermons of Jane Austen's cousin Edward Cooper. (See my "*Pride and Prejudice* and Edward Cooper's *Sermons*," *Notes and Queries*, 211 [1966]: 182.) And W. H.

suggested that the first proposal scene in *Pride and Prejudice* was influenced to a large extent by the scenes in *Cecilia* in which Mortimer Delvile states his objections to a marriage with Cecilia, and there are similarities between the scene in which Mrs. Delvile prevails on Cecilia to give Mortimer up and the scene in which Lady Catherine de Bourgh descends on Elizabeth Bennet. There are, however, a number of significant points of resemblance between *Pride and Prejudice* and novels other than *Cecilia*. In some respects the situation of Fanny Burney's Evelina is closer to that of Elizabeth Bennet than Cecilia's is. Both Elizabeth and Evelina are relatively poor in addition to being inferior in rank to their heroes, while Cecilia is rich, and both are surrounded by sets of vulgar relatives who embarrass them in the presence of their lovers. Moreover, some specific scenes in *Pride and Prejudice* are almost certainly based on similar scenes in *Evelina*. Some others, on the other hand, would seem to have their originals in *Sir Charles Grandison*. I believe that in her novel Jane Austen is not rewriting *Cecilia*, but manipulating a character type and a situation made familiar to her audience in various novels by Richardson and Fanny Burney—and in numerous works by their imitators as well. The relationship between *Evelina* and *Pride and Prejudice* has never been fully explored; and since it seems in some respects rewarding to compare Jane Austen's Mr. Darcy to Fanny Burney's Lord Orville, I shall rely primarily on *Evelina* to illustrate Fanny Burney's treatment of the patrician hero.

Welpley, in "Pride and Prejudice," *Notes and Queries*, 196 (1951): 93, remarks that the expression is used in *Sir Charles Grandison*. See also above note 11 to the introduction.

While all of Fanny Burney's heroes resemble Richardson's patrician hero somewhat, Lord Orville is Sir Charles Grandison writ small. He is "a picture of perfection," a paragon among men—at least in the eyes of his heroine and his author. Evelina describes him as "one who seemed formed as a pattern for his fellow creatures, as a model of perfection" (p. 280). He is handsome, wellborn, rich, wise. "His conversation," Evelina gushes after her first encounter with him, "was sensible and spirited; his air and address were open and noble; his manners gentle, attentive, and infinitely engaging; his person is all elegance, and his countenance, the most animated and expressive I have ever seen" (p. 33).

The relationship between Orville and Evelina is much the same as that between Sir Charles Grandison and Harriet Byron. Evelina adores Orville from their first meeting, and she is fully convinced of her own inferiority. "That he should be so much my superior in every way, quite disconcerted me," she writes after their first dance together (p. 33). She cringes when she learns that he has referred to her as "a poor weak girl" and is "grateful for his attention" even after she believes that he has insulted her with a dishonorable proposal. Orville, like Sir Charles, is regarded as an oracular "monitor" by his heroine, and Evelina seeks, and is delighted to receive, his counsel. "'There is no young creature, my Lord, who so greatly wants, or so earnestly wishes for, the advice and assistance of her friends, as I do,'" she says to him on one occasion (p. 331), and Orville quickly becomes a substitute for her absent guardian. It is he who arranges an interview with Mr. Macartney for her at Bristol, who persuades the repentant Sir John Belmont to receive her—and who, later on, magnanimously disposes of half of her fortune to provide for Macartney and the onetime Miss Belmont. Like Harriet Byron, Evelina is overcome with gratitude when her hero finally proposes to her. "To be loved by Lord Orville," she writes, "to be the honoured choice of his noble heart,—my happiness seemed too infinite to be borne, and I wept, even bitterly I wept, from the excess of joy which overpowered me" (p. 383). And just before her marriage she writes to Mr. Villars: "Oh my dearest Sir, the thankfulness of my heart I must pour forth at our meeting ... when my noble-minded, my beloved Lord Orville, presents to you the highly-honoured and thrice-happy Evelina" (p. 438).

The relationship between the heroes and heroines of *Cecilia* and *Camilla* is similar to that between Orville and Evelina. In both of the later novels a most exemplary hero stoops to marry, and there is doubt as to whether the heroine will be found worthy of his hand. Both Cecilia and Camilla are "in love and in some doubt of a return" during a considerable part of their histories; both are left in suspense to await the approval of their heroes—and that of their heroes' advisors as well. And the reader reacts to all of Fanny Burney's first three novels in much the same way that he reacts to Richardson's "picture of perfection" Sir Charles Grandison, and his sycophant-heroine, Harriet Byron. One is amused and irritated by the relationship between hero and heroine: he longs for an Evelina who will tell Orville that her conversations with Mr. Macartney are her own affair; a Camilla who will tell Edgar Mandlebert to send Dr. Marchmont packing; a Cecilia who will tell the Delvile family what they really are. Such longings were apparently not felt by many novelists of the day, however, for the

Burney-Richardson character type and situation were often imitated in the minor literature of the period. In Thomas Hull's *The History of Sir William Harrington*, for example (1771), the exemplary Lord C——, nobly born, extremely wealthy, and "as perfect as a human being can be" in person, mind, and character, is obviously modeled on Sir Charles Grandison. And Mr. Charlemont, the hero of a novel by Anna Maria Porter entitled *The Lake of Killarney* (1804), is "a young Apollo," "the god of his sex," and the son of a lord. Rose, a dependent in a family of Charlemont's acquaintance, loves him desperately, but is by no means unaware of his vast superiority to her. At one point in the novel, in an episode that seems to have been inspired by the scene in *Cecilia* in which Mrs. Delvile warns Cecilia to beware of falling in love with Delvile, Rose is cross-examined by an older woman who is a friend of Charlemont's family. "'If nothing else were wanting to crush presumptuous hopes on my part,'" Rose replies, "'. . . the difference in our rank, our birth, our fortune, would place them beyond all doubt. Mr. Charlemont is . . . a prize, for which all his equals may contend.'" [6] Similar heroes, often similarly difficult of attainment to admiring heroines, are to be found in numerous other works of Jane Austen's day. The patrician hero, clearly, was a character type that Jane Austen's audience could readily identify.

Jane Austen must have been as much amused by the all-conquering heroes and too humble heroines of Richardson and Fanny Burney and their followers as many later readers have been, for in the juvenile sketch entitled "Jack and

[6] Anna Maria Porter, *The Lake of Killarney* (London, 1804), vol. 1, chap. 4, p. 219. Jane Austen mentions this novel in a letter of October 24, 1808 (*Letters*, pp. 58–59).

Alice" she reduces the patrician hero to absurdity with gusto. Charles Adams, in that sketch, is the most exaggerated "picture of perfection" conceivable. He is a young man "of so dazzling a Beauty that none but Eagles could look him in the Face" (*Minor Works*, p. 13). On one occasion, indeed, when he attends a masquerade disguised as the sun, the reader is told that "the Beams that darted from his Eyes were like those of that glorious Luminary tho' infinitely superior. So strong were they that no one dared venture within half a mile of them" (*Minor Works*, p. 13).[7] (The continual references in "Jack and Alice" to the brilliance of Charles' countenance are probably specific allusions to *Sir Charles Grandison*: Richardson repeatedly describes Sir Charles in similar language.)[8] But the beauties of Charles Adams' person, striking as they are, are nothing to those of his mind. As he tells us himself:

"... I imagine my Manners & Address to be of the most polished kind; there is a certain elegance, a peculiar sweetness in them that I never saw equalled, & cannot describe— Partiality aside, I am certainly more accomplished in every Language, every Science, every Art and every thing than any other person in Europe. My temper is even, my virtues innumerable, my self unparalelled." (*Minor Works*, p. 25)

[7] The masquerade at which Charles shines is probably a humorous reminiscence of a similar scene in *Cecilia*, as I have pointed out in "Fanny Burney's *Cecilia* and Jane Austen's 'Jack and Alice,'" *English Language Notes*, 3 (1965): 40–42.

[8] As E. E. Duncan-Jones points out in "Notes on Jane Austen," *Notes and Queries*, 196 (1951): 14–16. Numbers of heroes in the minor fiction of the period, however, among them Lord C—— in *The History of Sir William Harrington* and Mr. Charlemont in *The Lake of Killarney*, are similarly described.

The superciliousness and conceit that readers, in spite of Richardson's and Fanny Burney's insistence on their modesty, cannot help attributing to Sir Charles Grandison or Orville or Delvile, becomes the very essence of Charles Adams' being; the kind of praise that Richardson and Fanny Burney heap on their heroes is most liberally bestowed by Charles on himself. And just as Charles himself is a burlesque version of the too perfect Burney-Richardson hero, so he is provided with two heroines who are ten times more inferior, and twenty times more devoted to him, than Evelina and Cecilia and Harriet Byron are to their heroes. Charles is the owner of the "principal estate" in the neighborhood in which the lovely Lucy lives, and Lucy adores him. She is the daughter of a tailor and the niece of an alehouse-keeper, and she is "'fearful that tho' possessed of Youth, Beauty, Wit & Merit, and tho' the probable Heiress of my Aunts House & business'" Charles may think her "'deficient in Rank, & in being so, unworthy of his hand'" (*Minor Works*, p. 21). Screwing up her courage, however, she writes him a "'very kind letter, offering him with great tenderness my hand & heart,'" but, to her sorrow, receives "'an angry & peremptory refusal'" from the unapproachable young man (*Minor Works*, p. 21). Alice Johnson, the titular heroine of the novel, is also infatuated with Charles. Although, like the rest of her family, Alice is "a little addicted to the Bottle & the Dice," she hopes, after she has inherited a considerable estate, to be found worthy of him. But when Alice's father proposes the match to him, Charles declares:

> "... what do you mean by wishing me to marry your Daughter? ... Your Daughter Sir, is neither sufficiently beautifull sufficiently amiable, sufficiently witty, nor sufficiently rich for me—. I expect nothing more in my

wife than my wife will find in me—Perfection." (*Minor Works*, pp. 25–26)

Fortunately, Alice is able to find consolation in her bottle, and fortunately there is a feminine "picture of perfection"— the outrageously exemplary Lady Williams—in the neighborhood of Pammydiddle for Charles to marry. "Jack and Alice," however, was not Jane Austen's only attack on the patrician hero. There is a good deal of Charles Adams in her Mr. Darcy.

II

Darcy's actual circumstances are not an exaggeration of those of the patrician hero, as Charles Adams' are. In fact Jane Austen seems at times to be uncritically borrowing the popular Burney-Richardson character type and situation in *Pride and Prejudice*—altering them, if at all, only by toning them down a bit. Mr. Darcy is not the "picture of perfection" that Sir Charles Grandison is, but he shares many of the advantages of Sir Charles and Lord Orville, including a "fine, tall person, handsome features, noble mien . . . and ten thousand a year" (p. 10). He has a mind that even Elizabeth Bennet, his severest critic, can respect. "His understanding and temper," she admits when there seems to be little likelihood of their ever marrying, "though unlike her own, would have answered all her wishes . . . and from his judgment, information, and knowledge of the world, she must have received benefit . . ." (p. 312). Darcy is not as powerful and important as Sir Charles Grandison, but he is the owner of a large estate and a giver, and withholder, of clerical livings. He marries a woman who, like Evelina, is embarrassed by the inferiority of some of her nearest connections, although even Mrs. Bennet can scarcely approach the supreme vulgarity of a Madame Duval.

But Darcy is a Charles Adams in spirit, if not in circumstances.[9] It is his exaggerated conception of the importance of his advantages, his supercilious determination "'to think well of myself, and meanly of others'" who are not so fortunate that causes him at times to sound very much like a caricature of the Burney-Richardson hero. He may not expect to have to address "an angry & peremptory refusal" to a fawning, lovelorn Elizabeth Bennet; but during Elizabeth's visit at Netherfield he is anxious lest, by devoting so much of his conversation to her, he may have been encouraging her to hope for the honor of his hand. On the eve of her departure from Netherfield, the reader is told:

> He wisely resolved to be particularly careful that no sign of admiration should *now* escape him, nothing that could elevate her with the hope of influencing his felicity; sensible that if such an idea had been suggested, his behavior during the last day must have material weight in confirming or crushing it. Steady to his purpose, he scarcely spoke ten words to her through the whole of Saturday, and though they were at one time left by themselves for half an hour, he adhered most conscientiously to his book, and would not even look at her. (p. 60)

The idea of a proposal which is humiliating to a heroine may come from *Cecilia*. But the language of Darcy's first

---

[9] Compare the opinion of F. W. Bradbrook (*Jane Austen and Her Predecessors*, pp. 96–97) regarding Jane Austen's treatment of the Burney-Richardson hero. Bradbrook feels that Jane Austen "accepts Fanny Burney's conception of the hero" although he does suggest that she "deflates" Darcy somewhat.

proposal to Elizabeth sounds like something that might have come from Charles Adams' lips, rather than the gallant, ardent language of a Delvile.[10] During Darcy's proposal, the reader is told: "His sense of her inferiority—of its being a degradation—of the family obstacles which judgment had always opposed to inclination, were dwelt on with a warmth which seemed due to the consequence he was wounding, but was very unlikely to recommend his suit" (p. 189). And when Elizabeth rebukes him, he declares himself not to be "'ashamed of the feelings I related. They were natural and just. Could you expect me to rejoice in the inferiority of your connections? To congratulate myself on the hope of relations, whose condition in life is so decidedly beneath my own?'" (p. 192).

On two occasions, Darcy is specifically a caricature of Fanny Burney's Lord Orville. The scene at the Meryton assembly in which Darcy makes his rude remarks about Elizabeth Bennet is a parody of Lord Orville's unfavorable first impression of Evelina.[11] In *Evelina*, shortly after Orville and Evelina have had their first dance together, Miss Mirvan overhears a conversation between Orville and Sir Clement Willoughby. She repeats the conversation to Evelina, much to Evelina's mortification, and the scene is recorded in a letter to Mr. Villars:

> ... a very gay-looking man [Sir Clement Willoughby, as the reader learns later] stepping hastily up to him, cried,

[10] Bradbrook (*Jane Austen and Her Predecessors*, pp. 127–132) compares the first proposal scene to one in Sir Egerton Brydges' *Mary de Clifford*, and suggests other parallels between Brydges' work and Jane Austen's.

[11] In "A Critical Theory of Jane Austen's Writings," pt. 1, *Scrutiny*, 10 (1941): 61–87, Q. D. Leavis recognizes the similarity between the two scenes.

"Why, my Lord, what have you done with your lovely partner?"

"Nothing!" answered Lord Orville, with a smile and a shrug.

"By Jove," cried the man, "she is the most beautiful creature I ever saw in my life!"

Lord Orville, as well he might, laughed, but answered, "Yes; a pretty modest-looking girl."

"O my Lord!" cried the madman, "she is an angel!"

"A *silent* one," returned he.

"Why ay, my Lord, how stands she as to that? She looks all intelligence and expression."

"A poor weak girl!" answered Lord Orville, shaking his head. (p. 39)

In Darcy's remarks about Elizabeth at the Meryton assembly, Orville's gentle mockery becomes supercilious rudeness. Mr. Bingley enters into conversation with Darcy on the merits of the various ladies at the assembly, hoping to persuade his friend to dance. Like Sir Clement Willoughby, Bingley praises the heroine: Elizabeth, he declares, is "'very pretty, and I dare say, very agreeable'"; and he proposes that Darcy ask her to dance. Darcy replies: "'She is tolerable; but not handsome enough to tempt *me*; and I am in no humour at present to give consequence to young ladies who are slighted by other men'" (p. 12).

A second ballroom scene in *Evelina* is also parodied in *Pride and Prejudice*. At one point in *Evelina* Sir Clement Willoughby, who is determined to punish the heroine for pretending that Lord Orville is to be her partner in a dance for which Sir Clement wished to engage her, conducts her to Lord Orville and presents him with her hand. Evelina writes:

...—he suddenly seized my hand, saying, "think, my Lord, what must be my reluctance to resign this fair hand to your Lordship!"

In the same instant, Lord Orville took it of him; I coloured violently, and made an effort to recover it. "You do me too much honour, Sir," cried he, (with an air of gallantry, pressing it to his lips before he let it go) "however, I shall be happy to profit by it, if this lady," (turning to Mrs. Mirvan) "will permit me to seek for her party."

To compel him thus to dance, I could not endure, and eagerly called out, "By no means,—not for the world!—I must beg—. . . . (pp. 51–52)

Orville, with true politeness, attempts to help Evelina recover from her confusion. Darcy, "all politeness," as Elizabeth ironically describes him, signifies his willingness to oblige Elizabeth Bennet with a dance when Elizabeth is placed in a similarly embarrassing situation at Sir William Lucas' ball.[12] Sir William and Darcy are conversing. Elizabeth approaches them and Sir William, "struck with the notion of doing a very gallant thing," calls out to her:

"My dear Miss Eliza, why are you not dancing?— Mr. Darcy, you must allow me to present this young lady to you as a very desirable partner. —You cannot refuse to dance, I am sure, when so much beauty is before you." And taking her hand, he would have given it to Mr. Darcy, who, though extremely surprised, was not unwilling to receive it, when she instantly drew back, and said with some discomposure to Sir William,

"Indeed, Sir, I have not the least intention of dancing.— I entreat you not to suppose that I moved this way in order to beg for a partner."

Mr. Darcy with grave propriety requested to be allowed

---

12 Of course, as Reuben Brower, in *The Fields of Light* (New York: Oxford University Press, 1951), pp. 168–169, points out, the reader sees this scene largely through the eyes of the prejudiced Elizabeth Bennet. Darcy is actually happy to dance with Elizabeth, although his manner of expressing himself is not as gallant as it might be.

the honour of her hand; but in vain. Elizabeth was determined; nor did Sir William at all shake her purpose by his attempt at persuasion.

"You excel so much in the dance, Miss Eliza, that it is cruel to deny me the happiness of seeing you; and though this gentleman dislikes the amusement in general, he can have no objection, I am sure, to oblige us for one half hour."

"Mr. Darcy is all politeness," said Elizabeth, smiling. (p. 26)

Mr. Darcy is a complex human being rather than a mere vehicle for satire such as Charles Adams. Nevertheless, I think it is likely that Darcy has somewhere in his ancestry a parody-figure similar to the ones in which Jane Austen's juvenilia abound. Such a theory of Darcy's origins is consistent with generally accepted assumptions about the development of Jane Austen's first three novels from prototypes. It is not unreasonable to assume that *Pride and Prejudice*, as well as *Sense and Sensibility*, grew, through a process of revision, from an original containing large amounts of satire of literature to a differently oriented work. Moreover, the theory helps to account for a feature of *Pride and Prejudice* that has been noted by a number of readers: the inconsistency between the Darcy of the first ballroom scene and the man whom Elizabeth marries at the end of the novel. It is often said that the transition between the conceited and arrogant young man of the book's early chapters and the polite gentleman whom Elizabeth loves and admires is too great and too abrupt to be completely credible.[13] Several critics have defended Jane Austen, showing among

---

[13] See, for example, the comments on Darcy in Mary Lascelles' *Jane Austen and Her Art*, pp. 22 and 162, and Marvin Mudrick's complaints about the change in Darcy's character in his *Irony as Defense and Discovery*, pp. 117–119.

other things that some of Darcy's conversation can be interpreted in various ways, and that the reader's reactions to him are often conditioned by the fact that he is seen largely through the eyes of the prejudiced Elizabeth.[14] But even these theories do not account for all the things in *Pride and Prejudice* that trouble readers. Darcy's remark about Elizabeth at the Meryton assembly, for instance, remains almost unbelievably boorish, and there is no reason to believe that Elizabeth has misunderstood it.[15] His fears lest he should be encouraging Elizabeth to fall in love with him during the visit at Netherfield, the extraordinarily haughty language of his first proposal, and other such things remain stumbling blocks to the reader's acceptance of the later Darcy. The three things just mentioned could have originated in parody of the patrician hero, as has been shown. If one postulates an origin in parody for Darcy and assumes that, like many characters in Jane Austen's novels, he was subjected to a refining process, these and perhaps others of the early, exaggerated displays of rudeness and conceit can be accounted for, if not excused, as traces of the original purely parodic figure that Jane Austen was not able to manage with complete success.

Regardless of its origins, *Pride and Prejudice*, even as it stands, is in many respects a subtly humorous reflection on

[14] See the chapters on *Pride and Prejudice* in Brower's *The Fields of Light*, pp. 164–181, and in Babb's *The Fabric of Dialogue*, pp. 115–118, and Charles J. McCann's "Setting and Character in *Pride and Prejudice*," *Nineteenth Century Fiction*, 19 (1964): 65–75.

[15] Compare, however, Philip Drew's "A Significant Incident in *Pride and Prejudice*," *Nineteenth Century Fiction*, 13 (1958): 356–368, in which Darcy's asperity toward the opposite sex at the assembly is explained as the result of temporary chagrin engendered by his sister's affair with Wickham.

Richardson and Fanny Burney and their patrician heroes. In addition to Darcy's role as a comically treated Orville or Sir Charles Grandison, Lady Catherine de Bourgh is a reminiscence of Mrs. Delvile in *Cecilia* or Dr. Marchmont in *Camilla*, a humorous version of the kindly but mistaken friend who frowns upon the patrician hero's intended bride. And the scene in which she attempts to persuade Elizabeth not to marry Darcy is an exaggeration of what is potentially ridiculous in similar situations in *Cecilia*—not, as R. Brimley Johnson and others have suggested, a refined imitation. Mrs. Delvile is Mortimer's mother and exercises, according to Cecilia, an almost maternal prerogative upon Cecilia herself. Cecilia is grateful—exaggeratedly, unnecessarily grateful, many readers feel—to Mrs. Delvile for that lady's interest in her and for her kindness in providing her with a home during part of her minority. Mrs. Delvile has as much right as anyone could have to interfere in the love affair between Mortimer and Cecilia. And when she persuades Cecilia not to marry Mortimer, although what she says is prideful and humiliating to Cecilia, her language, at least, is kind and respectful. "'Acquit me, I beg,'" she says to Cecilia at one point,

> "of any intentional insolence, and imagine not that in speaking highly of my own family, I mean to depreciate yours: on the contrary, I know it to be respectable, I know, too, that were it the lowest in the kingdom, the first might envy it that it gave birth to such a daughter."

And a little later she declares:

> "You were just, indeed, the woman he had least chance to resist, you were precisely the character to seize his very soul. To a softness the most fatally alluring, you join a

dignity which rescues from their own contempt even the most humble of your admirers. You seem born to have all the world wish your exaltation, and no part of it murmur at your superiority. Were any obstacle but this insuperable one in the way, should nobles, nay should princes offer their daughters to my election, I would reject without murmuring the most magnificent proposals, and take in triumph to my heart my son's nobler choice!"[16]

Lady Catherine is Darcy's aunt, and she hardly knows Elizabeth. Her attempt to prevent Elizabeth's and Darcy's marriage, her arrogant language and the manner in which she taxes Elizabeth with ingratitude, on the strength of having invited her to Rosings several times in the past, are a parody of the situation in *Cecilia*. Again, several scholars have remarked that Mr. Collins, with his moralizing and his flattery of his patroness and her family, parodies the didactic and obsequious clergymen found in Richardson's and Fanny Burney's works.[17] Darcy's relationship with Mr. Bingley is humorously reminiscent of Sir Charles Grandison and the friends who continually depend on him for advice and assistance. Richardson's supercompetent hero was notable for his propensity to manage the lives and loves of his

[16] Fanny Burney, *Cecilia* (London, 1893), vol. 3, bk. 8, chap. 3, p. 22, and chap. 4, p. 37.

[17] For fuller discussion of this point see Alan D. McKillop, "Critical Realism in *Northanger Abbey*," in *From Jane Austen to Joseph Conrad: Essays in Honor of James T. Hillhouse*, eds. Robert C. Rathburn and Martin Steinmann, Jr. (Minneapolis: University of Minnesota Press, 1958), p. 37; B. C. Southam's "Jane Austen and *Clarissa*," *Notes and Queries*, 208 (1963): 191–192; and Henrietta Ten Harmsel's *A Study in Fictional Conventions*, pp. 83–84. For another aspect of Collins' literary background, see J. M. S. Tompkins' *The Popular Novel in England, 1770–1800* (Lincoln, Neb.: University of Nebraska Press, 1961), p. 132.

friends. Darcy, to the reader's and Elizabeth Bennet's amusement, domineers over the spineless Bingley, arranging and rearranging Bingley's love life, and at one point officiously separating him from the amiable and disinterested young woman whom Bingley truly loves. Darcy is provided with a mock Evelina or Harriet Byron in Miss Bingley, who is all too obviously willing to play the role of the patrician hero's female adorer in order to become the mistress of Pemberley. "'Now be sincere'"; Elizabeth says to Darcy toward the end of the novel, "'did you admire me for my impertinence?...'"

> "The fact is, that you were sick of civility, of deference, of officious attention. You were disgusted with the women who were always speaking and looking, and thinking for *your* approbation alone. I roused, and interested you, because I was so unlike *them*... and in your heart, you thoroughly despised the persons who so assiduously courted you." (p. 380)

And it is not difficult to see whom she has chiefly in mind. The flattery Evelina and Harriet Byron unconsciously heap upon their heroes, their willingness to take their young men's pronouncements as law, become Miss Bingley's determined and obvious toadeating: when she is not praising Darcy's library or his sister, she is defending his views on the subject of feminine accomplishments or inviting his comments on the company at Sir William Lucas' ball.

Most important, while Miss Bingley is an exaggeration and distortion of qualities in Evelina or Harriet Byron, Elizabeth Bennet plays the role of an anti-Evelina in the novel's satiric pattern.[18] Throughout most of the novel she

[18] Q. D. Leavis ("Critical Theory," pt. 1) adopts a view of Elizabeth's origins that is somewhat similar to my own, holding that much

acts in a manner directly contrary to the way in which one would expect a heroine of Richardson's or Fanny Burney's to behave.[19] While the would-be Harriet Byron, Miss Bingley, courts Darcy in the traditional manner, Elizabeth makes him the butt of her wit and the prime target of her attacks on snobbery and class consciousness. "'My behavior to *you*,'" she says to him toward the end of the novel, "'was at least always bordering on the uncivil, and I never spoke to you without rather wishing to give you pain than not'" (p. 380). While he worries lest he should have encouraged her to hope for the honor of his hand, she is regarding him as "only the man who made himself agreeable no where, and who had not thought her handsome enough to dance with" (p. 23). Instead of being overwhelmed with gratitude when he proposes to her, she prefaces her refusal by saying: "'. . . if I could *feel* gratitude, I would now thank

of *Pride and Prejudice* was originally a satire on *Cecilia* and that Elizabeth is an "anti-Cecilia." She feels, however, that Darcy is simply a refined imitation of Mortimer Delvile, "Delvile with the minimum of inside necessary to make plausible his conduct"—an opinion with which, of course, I disagree; I believe, too, Elizabeth is an antitype to Harriet Byron, Evelina, and a number of other heroines as well as to Cecilia, and not simply a vehicle for satire of one particular novel.

[19] According to Henrietta Ten Harmsel, in the chapter on *Pride and Prejudice* in her *A Study in Fictional Conventions*, Elizabeth is an antitype to conventional heroines in some ways other than the ones I am about to mention. She is a forceful, vigorous character, where the conventional heroine is passive. Where the traditional heroine is outstandingly beautiful and accomplished, Elizabeth is only "tolerably" handsome, and far from proficient in the feminine "accomplishments" of the period. The typical heroine of the Burney-Richardson tradition is a moral paragon (it would seem that Fanny Burney's Camilla is a notable exception to this rule), whereas Elizabeth's fallibility is stressed. Miss Ten Harmsel also feels that Elizabeth's originality is emphasized by contrast with Jane Bennet, who is a heroine of the conventional stamp.

you. But I cannot—I have never desired your good opinion, and you have certainly bestowed it most unwillingly'" (p. 190). And she goes on to tax him with "arrogance," "conceit," and a "selfish disdain for the feelings of others" (p. 193), and to accuse him of being snobbish and overbearing in his interference with Jane and Bingley and of abusing the power he holds over Wickham. Even when she and Darcy are reconciled she laughs, though only to herself, at his casual assumption of the right to arrange and rearrange his friend Bingley's love affairs. When Darcy described the manner in which he sent Bingley back to Jane Bennet with his blessing, "Elizabeth could not help smiling at his easy manner of directing his friend. . . . [She] longed to observe that Mr. Bingley had been a most delightful friend; so easily guided that his worth was invaluable; but she checked herself" (p. 371). Again, Elizabeth answers Lady Catherine de Bourgh's demand that she renounce Darcy in a manner calculated to warm the hearts of readers irritated by Cecilia Beverly's deference to Mrs. Delvile's pride and prejudice:

> "Allow me to say, Lady Catherine, that the arguments with which you have supported this extraordinary application, have been as frivolous as the application was illjudged. You have widely mistaken my character, if you think I can be worked on by such persuasions as these. How far your nephew might approve of your interference in *his* affairs, I cannot tell; but you have certainly no right to concern yourself in mine. I must beg, therefore, to be importuned no farther on the subject." (p. 357)

> "I am . . . resolved to act in that manner, which will, in my own opinion, constitute my happiness, without reference to *you*, or to any person so wholly unconnected with me. . . .

"Neither duty, nor honour, nor gratitude . . . have any possible claim on me, in the present instance. No principle of either, would be violated by my marriage with Mr. Darcy. And with regard to the resentment of his family, or the indignation of the world, if the former *were* excited by his marrying me, it would not give me one moment's concern—and the world in general would have too much sense to join in the scorn." (p. 358)[20]

In earlier stages of the novel's growth, probably Lady Catherine, Mr. Bingley, and Miss Bingley were more exaggerated and distorted versions of their prototypes in eighteenth- and early nineteenth-century literature than they are at present. Elizabeth Bennet was merely an antitype to the Burney-Richardson sycophantic heroine; Darcy, a caricature of the patrician hero. Later, although she retained an element of ironic imitation, Jane Austen refined her characters, transforming them from mere vehicles for satire into human beings interesting in their own right as well as because of their relationship to their literary prototypes.[21] And, as the remainder of this chapter implies, she also changed her attitude toward her patrician hero and her anti-Evelina, and accordingly altered her treatment of Darcy drastically and made Elizabeth, as well as Darcy, a target for

[20] Compare Ten Harmsel, *A Study in Fictional Conventions*, pp. 90–91. Miss Ten Harmsel notes the similarity between Lady Catherine de Bourgh and Mrs. Delvile, but feels that there is a more marked similarity between Lady Catherine's encounter with Elizabeth Bennet and the scene in *Pamela* where Lady Davers abuses Pamela for having captivated Mr. B——.

[21] Another view of the novel's origins and development is found in B. C. Southam's *Jane Austen's Literary Manuscripts*, pp. 59–62, where it is suggested that *Pride and Prejudice* was originally a satire, in epistolary form, on the theme of "first impressions" that was so prevalent in the literature of Jane Austen's day.

her irony. Theories about the development of the novel aside, however, the fact remains that *Pride and Prejudice* in its final form is not simply, as critics have suggested, an imitation of the work of Jane Austen's fellow novelists. It is, in part at least, an attack on Richardson and Fanny Burney and their patrician heroes.

III

Jane Austen thoroughly humbles her patrician hero. Darcy is subjected to a series of what Mrs. Bennet would call "set-downs" at the hands of the anti-Evelina, Elizabeth Bennet; and through his love for Elizabeth, and the shock he receives from her behavior, he comes to see himself as he really is and to repent of his pomposity and pride. Toward the end of the novel Darcy is forced to admit to Elizabeth:

> "I have been a selfish being all my life, in practice, though not in principle. As a child I was taught what was *right*, but I was not taught to correct my temper. I was given good principles, but left to follow them in pride and conceit . . . my parents . . . allowed, encouraged, almost taught me to be selfish and overbearing, to care for none beyond my own family circle, to think meanly of all the rest of the world, to *wish* at least to think meanly of their sense and worth compared with my own. Such I was, from eight to eight and twenty; and such I might still have been but for you, dearest, loveliest Elizabeth! What do I not owe you! You taught me a lesson, hard indeed at first, but most advantageous. By you, I was properly humbled. I came to you without a doubt of my reception. You shewed me how insufficient were all my pretensions to please a woman worthy of being pleased." (p. 369)

But Darcy's humiliation and attainment of self-knowledge do not constitute the whole story of *Pride and Prejudice*: Jane Austen does not allow her anti-Evelina to rout her patrician hero completely.

In discussing *Sense and Sensibility* it was noted that an ironic reversal of attitude toward the traditional deluded "sensibility" heroine and her sensible counterpart takes place in that novel. Something a bit similar happens in *Pride and Prejudice*, in Jane Austen's treatment of Darcy and his relationship to Elizabeth Bennet. Once Darcy has been humbled, Jane Austen turns her irony on Elizabeth. She shows that Elizabeth, in her resentment of Darcy's conscious superiority, has exaggerated his faults and failed to see that there is much in him that is good. Elizabeth proves to have been blind and prejudiced in her views on the relationship between Darcy and Wickham, too willing to accept Wickham's stories because they so nicely confirmed her own feelings about Darcy. When she reads the letter that follows Darcy's first proposal, she is forced to admit that her resentment has led her to be foolish and unjust. After reading the letter,

> She grew absolutely ashamed of herself.—Of neither Darcy nor Wickham could she think, without feeling that she had been blind, partial, prejudiced, absurd.
> "How despicably have I acted!" she cried.... "Had I been in love, I could not have been more wretchedly blind. But vanity, not love, has been my folly.—Pleased with the preference of one, and offended by the neglect of the other, on the very beginning of our acquaintance, I have courted prepossession and ignorance, and driven reason away, where either were concerned. Till this moment, I never knew myself." (p. 208)

Again, until Darcy's letter shocks her into self-knowledge, Elizabeth has seen Darcy's interference in the affair between Jane and Bingley only as an instance of coldhearted snobbery on Darcy's part. Reading Darcy's letter, and considering Jane's disposition, Elizabeth is forced to admit that Darcy's view of the affair, his belief that Jane was little more than a complacent pawn in her mother's matrimonial game, is not unjustified. Darcy's interference, Elizabeth must admit, was motivated not merely by snobbery, but by concern for his guileless friend's welfare as well. With her eyes thus opened, Elizabeth comes to see later in the novel that Darcy's position and fortune, and his pride in them, can be forces for good as well as sources of snobbery and authoritarianism. Seeing Pemberley, and hearing his housekeeper's praise of Darcy's conduct as a brother and a landlord, she learns that Darcy's position is a trust and a responsibility, and that his not unjustifiable self-respect leads to a code of conduct worthy of admiration. And in his action in the Lydia-Wickham affair she is provided with an impressive and gratifying instance of his power to do good and his sense of responsibility. At the end of the novel Jane Austen's anti-Evelina is defending her patrician hero. "'I love him,'" Elizabeth says of Darcy to the astounded Mr. Bennet. "'Indeed, he has no improper pride'" (p. 376).

As noted earlier, a pattern of "art-nature" symbolism in *Pride and Prejudice* served to add depth of suggestion, for Jane Austen's early nineteenth-century audience, to the novel's love plot. At the beginning of the story Darcy is the representative of a bias toward "art," and an excessive class pride, and Elizabeth is the exponent of "nature" and aggressive individualism. In the course of the novel their mental and temperamental propensities are modified somewhat, and their marriage at the conclusion of the story is a union between a reasonable degree of "art" and a desirable degree of "nature." Jane Austen's treatment of the figure here called the patrician hero serves a similar purpose and follows a similar pattern. One cannot, of course, assume that Jane Austen thought of her Mr. Darcy as an "authority figure," in today's sense of the term, any more than one can assume that she considered *Pride and Prejudice* a treatise on the eighteenth-century "art-nature" antithesis. But she did expect the novel-reading audience for which she wrote to respond to her work on the basis of their impressions of the insufferable Sir Charles Grandisons and Lord Orvilles, the sycophantic Evelinas and Harriet Byrons, of noveldom. At the beginning of *Pride and Prejudice* Darcy is a pompous Burney-Richardson aristocrat, with many of the most disagreeable attributes of his literary progenitors as well as a representative of "art" and excessive class pride; Elizabeth is a determined anti-Evelina as well as a symbol for "nature" and aggressive individualism. The marriage at the end of the story joins a properly humbled patrician hero and an anti-Evelina who has also undergone a partial reformation.

In view of what has just been said, it is interesting to note that, paralleling Elizabeth's attainment of self-knowledge, there is a marked tendency on Jane Austen's part to cease laughing at the works of Richardson and Fanny Burney and even to imitate them rather obviously in the later chapters of *Pride and Prejudice*. At Pemberley, for instance, Darcy is allowed to behave toward Elizabeth with a marked tact and gallantry that is nonhumorously reminiscent of Sir Charles Grandison or Lord Orville. In the manner of Richardson's and Fanny Burney's heroes he takes over his heroine's affairs, rescuing Elizabeth and her family from imminent disgrace and providing for the erring Lydia.[22] Moreover, Jane Austen's audience might well have recognized some decidedly nonsatiric echoes of *Sir Charles Grandison* in the scenes in which Elizabeth visits Pemberley. Sir Charles, as one might expect, has excellent taste in landscaping. He "pretends not to level hills, or to force and distort nature; but to help it, as he finds it, without letting art be seen in his works, where he can possibly avoid it" (vol. 3, letter 23, p. 246). On his country estate he has a

> large and convenient house, . . . situated in a spacious park; which has several fine avenues leading to it.
>
> On the north side of the park flows a winding stream, that may well be called a river, abounding with trout and other fish; the current quickened by a noble cascade, which tumbles down its foaming waters from a rock, which is continued to some extent, in a ledge of rock-work, rudely disposed.
>
> The park is remarkable for its prospects, lawns, and rich-appearing clumps of trees of large growth. (vol. 7, letter 6, p. 30)

The Pemberley grounds are kept up with a similar regard for nature and timber, and there is even a similarly managed, artificially swelled trout stream. Pemberley House, the reader is told, was

> situated on the opposite side of a valley, into which the road with some abruptness wound. It was a large, handsome, stone building, standing well on rising ground, and backed by a ridge of high woody hills;—and in front, a stream of

[22] In the chapter on *Pride and Prejudice* in Marvin Mudrick's *Irony as Defense and Discovery*, Darcy's resemblance to conventional heroes in the latter part of the novel is interpreted as one of its failings.

some natural importance was swelled into greater, but without any artificial appearance. Its banks were neither formal, nor falsely adorned. Elizabeth was delighted. She had never seen a place for which nature had done more, or where natural beauty had been so little counteracted by an awkward taste. (p. 245)

Was Jane Austen thinking of Harriet Byron's tour of Sir Charles Grandison's property when she described Elizabeth Bennet's visit to Pemberley? Both Elizabeth and Harriet are conducted around magnificent but tastefully appointed houses and both talk to elderly, respectable housekeepers who praise their masters' kindness to servants and tenants. "'Don't your ladyship see,'" Sir Charles' housekeeper asks Harriet Byron, "'how all his servants love him as they attend him at table?... Indeed, madam, we all adore him; and have prayed morning, noon, and night, for his coming hither, and settling among us'" (vol. 7, letter 9, p. 52). Darcy's housekeeper laments the fact that he is not at Pemberley "so much as I could wish" (p. 248), and declares that "'he is the best landlord, and the best master... that ever lived. Not like the wild young men now-a-days, who think of nothing but themselves. There is not one of his tenants or servants but what will give him a good name'" (p. 249). Harriet and Elizabeth are both conducted around noble picture galleries, and both view pictures of their lovers with admiration during their tours. [23]

[23] The fact that the episodes in *Grandison* just mentioned had been imitated in the minor literature of the period strengthens my belief that Jane Austen's borrowings are purposeful. In Thomas Hull's *The History of Sir William Harrington*, for example, similar scenes occur when Lord C——'s bride reaches her new habitation. See *Harrington* (London, 1772), vol. 3, letter 52, pp. 1–7. Compare the suggestion of F. W. Bradbrook (*Jane Austen and Her Predecessors*, pp. 58–59) that

As Darcy becomes a modified but genuine Sir Charles Grandison, so does Elizabeth cease to resemble an aggressive anti-Evelina or Harriet Byron. She becomes more and more impressed with her patrician hero, more and more attracted to his many good qualities. Indeed, as she stands in the gallery at Pemberley, there is even a trace of Evelina-like gratitude in her thoughts, and she feels honored by the love of such a man as Darcy:

> As a brother, a landlord, a master, she considered how many people's happiness were in his guardianship!—How much of pleasure or pain it was in his power to bestow!—how much of good or evil must be done by him! Every idea that had been brought forward by the housekeeper was favourable to his character, and as she stood before the canvas, on which he was represented, and fixed his eyes upon herself, she thought of his regard with a deeper sentiment of gratitude than it had ever raised before; she remembered its warmth, and softened its impropriety of expression. (pp. 250–251)

Pride and Prejudice is a story about two complex, sensitive and often blindly wrongheaded "intricate characters" and their progress toward a better understanding of one another, the world, and themselves. The drama of Elizabeth's and Darcy's conflict and ultimate harmony is played out in the context of a symbolism based on the antithesis between "art" and "nature," in the comprehensive eighteenth-century sense of those terms. It is also referred at many points to the fiction of Jane Austen's day—particularly to her fellow novelists' handling of the figure

---

the descriptions of Pemberley may have been influenced by passages in William Gilpin's *Observations on the Mountains and Lakes of Cumberland and Westmorland*.

called here the patrician hero. It may be that Jane Austen's first response to the patrician hero was purely satiric and that later she refined and complicated her treatment of him; this would help to account for some of the flaws in Darcy's character to which most of her readers object. At any rate, *Pride and Prejudice* is something more than a much-improved imitation of the novels Jane Austen knew. It is a work in which she tumbles an eighteenth-century authority figure from the pedestal on which Richardson and Fanny Burney had placed him—and, with a gesture typical of both her vision of life and her artistic technique, then stoops to retrieve him from the dust. [24]

[24] Jane Austen, of course, uses the patrician hero elsewhere. Henry Tilney, wiser and wealthier than his heroine, and adored by her almost from the moment they meet, is a more nearly "straight" Burney-Richardson hero. In a later chapter it will be noted that Edmund Bertram, mentor and eventual lover of Fanny Price, receives a treatment somewhat similar to Darcy's.

4

Mansfield Park and Feminine " Accomplishments "

Mansfield Park is frequently interpreted as a novel in which warmth, wit, and moral and intellectual individualism, as displayed by the Crawfords, particularly Mary Crawford, are pitted against a stern conservatism of which Fanny Price, Sir Thomas Bertram, and Edmund Bertram are the exemplars.[1] Many readers have felt that although Jane Austen intended the Mansfield trio to win an uncontested victory, the Crawfords in fact carry the day. Fanny, Edmund, and Sir Thomas emerge as frigid prudes. The charm of Mary and Henry captivates the reader throughout the novel, and Jane Austen's insistence on their immorality fails to sway him. The conclusion of the novel, in which Henry Crawford seduces Maria Rushworth and Mary fails to see the enormity of the crime, is unsatisfying, a feeble

[1] The most vehement condemnation of the novel's alleged conservatism is the relevant chapter in Marvin Mudrick's *Irony as Defense and Discovery*. Even Lionel Trilling, who ably defends Jane Austen's novel in the chapter on *Mansfield Park* in *The Opposing Self*, does so by interpreting it as a temporary lapse in Jane Austen's faith in the individual, an assertion, similar to that of Wordsworth's *Resolution and Independence*, that the self can be preserved only through commitment to conventional conceptions of duty and morality.

excuse for disposing of characters who threaten to override Jane Austen's thesis.

This kind of interpretation seems to me to be less than just to *Mansfield Park*. In the first place, to assume that the moral positions of Fanny, Sir Thomas, and Edmund Bertram are closely similar is to misread the novel. Second, it is doubtful that any one of the Mansfield trio represents the novel's standard of moral excellence. Until the end of the story not one of the three has attained what Jane Austen calls self-knowledge, and its concomitant accuracy in moral perception. Fanny, admittedly, comes closer than either of the other two to being the moral center of the novel. Yet, she too has her faults: she is by no means intended to be the "picture of perfection" that many readers take her to be. Finally, viewed in proper perspective, the Crawfords, in spite of their charm, emerge convincingly as examples of a cold and shallow mentality and morality that Jane Austen justly condemns.

As I read *Mansfield Park*, a version of the eighteenth-century "art-nature" antithesis underlies the relationship between Fanny Price and the Bertram family. Here the antithesis takes the form of a contrast between what might be called the "worldly" and the "unworldly" virtues. Life at Mansfield, under the supervision of Sir Thomas Bertram, is characterized by "elegance, propriety, regularity, harmony": all of the relatively superficial qualities that are of value in the eyes of what Jane Austen's contemporaries called "the world"—fortune, manners, elegance—are to be found there. What is lacking is the warm, unselfish affection, the heartfelt piety, the emotional commitment to moral principles, of a Fanny Price. Fanny is the remedy for the spiritual malady with which the Bertrams are afflicted, and in welcoming Fanny as a daughter at the end of the novel, Sir Thomas is signifying that he has attained a degree of the self-knowledge that is the Austen character's goal. Yet there is much that Fanny must and does learn from the decorum and elegance of Mansfield. A similar pattern underlies the other major element in the plot of *Mansfield Park*, the relationship among Fanny, Edmund Bertram, and Mary Crawford. The Crawfords are presented as extreme cases of the same moral malady that prevails in the Mansfield family—not, as many critics believe, as characters who are opposed to the Bertrams in the moral scheme of the novel.

References to what Jane Austen's generation called feminine "accomplishments" occur frequently throughout the novel. These references help to give a clue to what Jane Austen was attempting to do in *Mansfield Park*. Consideration of the views of some of Jane Austen's contemporaries on the subject of "accomplishments" can perhaps provide a starting point from which to progress toward a clearer and more sympathetic understanding of the novel than one often encounters in modern criticism.

I

Although Rousseau's morals and politics were often vehemently attacked in the England of Jane Austen's day, much of the educational theory of his *Emile* seems to have gained a wide acceptance. Filtered through works such as Thomas Day's *Sanford and Merton*, many of Rousseau's theories became popular and influential. In the realm of female education, the plea for more practical, useful, "natural" education often took the form of an attack on the acquisition of "accomplishments" as the chief end of a woman's upbringing. In Jane Austen's day a number of people interested in the education of women were severely criticizing the kind of education which was designed to provide a young Miss Bingley with "'a thorough knowledge of music, singing, drawing, dancing, and the modern languages,'" a smattering of famous names and dates, and "'a certain something in her air and manner of walking, the tone of her voice, her address and expressions'" (*Pride and Prejudice*, p. 39). The "modern fine lady," would-be reformers felt, was an artificial and superficial creation; the inner woman was being neglected. Mothers and teachers, instead of concentrating on externals, should attempt to cultivate the hearts and the understandings of their charges. The *Edinburgh Review*, for example, expressed itself at length upon the subject of "accomplishments" in 1809:

> A decided and prevailing taste for one or another mode of education there must be. A century past, it was for housewifery,—now it is for accomplishments. . . . No woman of understanding and reflection can possibly conceive that she is doing justice to her children by such kind of education. The object is, to give children resources that will endure as long as life endures. . . . We do not mean to speak slightly of the fine arts, or to depreciate the good humor with which they are sometimes exhibited; but we appeal to any man, whether a little spirited and sensible conversation—displaying modestly, useful acquirements—and evincing rational curiosity, is not well worth the highest exertions of musical or graphical skill. A woman of accomplishments may entertain those who have the pleasure of knowing her for half an hour with great brilliancy; but a mind full of ideas, and with that elastic spring which the love of knowledge only can convey, is a perpetual source of exhilaration and amusement to all that come within its reach:—not

collecting its force into single and insulated achievements, like the efforts made in the fine arts—but diffusing, equally over the whole of existence, a calm pleasure—better loved as it is longer felt—and suitable to every variety and every period of life. Therefore, instead of hanging the understanding of a woman upon walls, or hearing it vibrate upon strings—instead of seeing it in clouds, or hearing it in the wind—we would make it the first spring and ornament of society, by enriching it with attainments upon which alone such power depends.[2]

Elizabeth Hamilton takes up the same theme in her *Popular Essays* (1812), as does Thomas Gisbourne in his *Enquiry into the Duties of the Female Sex* (1797).[3] Hannah More is much concerned with the deficiencies of the woman who is merely accomplished in her *Strictures on the Modern System of Female Education* (1799), a work that displays some important parallels to *Mansfield Park*.

"The great uses of study to a woman," according to Miss More, "are to enable her to regulate her own mind, and to be instrumental to the good of others."

To woman, therefore . . . I would recommend a predominance of those more sober studies, which not having

[2] *Edinburgh Review*, 15 (1809–1810): 306. The passage quoted occurs in a review of Thomas Broadhurst's *Advice to Young Ladies on the Improvement of the Mind* (1808).

[3] See Elizabeth Hamilton, *A Series of Popular Essays Illustrative of Principles Essentially Connected with the Improvement of the Understanding, the Imagination, and the Heart* (Edinburgh, 1813), especially essay 2, chap. 3. Jane Austen refers to Elizabeth Hamilton as "a respectable Writer" in a letter of November 6, 1813 (*Letters*, p. 372). See also Thomas Gisbourne, *An Enquiry into the Duties of the Female Sex* (London, 1798), especially pp. 55–58. R. W. Chapman (*Letters*, app. 5) concludes that a reference in an Austen letter of August 30, 1805 (*Letters*, p. 372) is probably to the *Enquiry*.

display for their object, may make her wise without vanity, happy without witnesses, and content without panegyrists. ... She should cultivate every study ... which will give her definite notions ... will lead her to think, ... will confer such a power of discrimination, that her judgment shall learn to reject what is dazzling, if it be not solid; and to prefer, not what is striking, or bright, or new, but what is just. (*Works*, vol. 1: *Strictures*, chap. 14, p. 363)

She warns against the "dangers arising from an excessive cultivation of the arts," at the expense of more substantial acquirements. She also opposes the fashionable system under which the study of history, geography, and other subjects is made to consist simply in the committing to memory of a smattering of facts, names, dates, and anecdotes suitable for drawing room use. Teachers who follow this practice are sacrificing their pupils' understandings to mere "external improvement." Information thus acquired not being

grounded in their minds by comment and conversation ... neither events, actions, characters nor chronology, fasten themselves on the understanding, but rather float in the memory as so many detached episodes, than contribute to form the mind and enrich the judgment of the reader. ... (*Strictures*, chap. 8, p. 343)

And she outlines a program of education aimed at teaching a young lady to think and feel as well as at cultivating the social graces. Learning, according to her program, becomes an exercise of the mind which tends to strengthen the judgment, the principles, and the feelings. In the study of history, for example,

the instructor will accustom the pupil not merely to store her memory with facts and anecdotes, and to ascertain

114

dates and epochs; but she will accustom her also to trace effects to their causes, to examine the secret springs of action, and accurately to observe the operation of the passions. (*Strictures*, chap. 9, p. 346)

And when the pupil studies geography and natural history,

the attention should be habitually turned to the goodness of Providence. . . . The reader may be led to admire the considerate goodness of Providence in having caused the spiry fir, whose slender foliage does not obstruct the beams of the sun, to grow in the dreary regions of the north, whose shivering inhabitants could spare none of its scanty rays; while in the torrid zone, the palm-tree, the plantain, and the banana, spread their umbrella leaves to break the almost intolerable fervors of a vertical sun. (*Strictures*, chap. 9, p. 349)

Theories about education and upbringing were also disseminated in fictional form, in tales in which girls whose educations had been directed toward the acquisition of accomplishments were contrasted with others who had received less superficial educations. In Hannah More's *Coelebs in Search of a Wife* (1808) Charles Coelebs sets out on his search armed with the following precepts:

I call education, not that which smothers a woman with accomplishments, but that which tends to consolidate a firm and regular system of character . . . not that which is made up of the shreds and patches of useless arts, but that which inculcates principles, polishes taste, regulates temper, cultivates reason, subdues the passions, directs the feelings, habituates to reflection, trains to self-denial, and, most especially, that which refers all actions, feelings, sentiments, tastes, and passions, to the love and fear of God.[4]

[4] Hannah More, *Coelebs in Search of a Wife* (London, 1808), vol. 1, chap. 2, p. 14. Jane Austen mentions *Coelebs* twice in the *Letters*

Charles meets several fashionable and accomplished but shallow young ladies and rejects them; he marries Lucilla Stanley, the daughter of a family who have taken pains to educate her more sensibly, and whose acquirements are less showy, but more solid and substantial.

A similar story, and one which is particularly interesting because of its resemblance to *Mansfield Park*, is Maria Edgeworth's "Mademoiselle Panache," which was mentioned earlier.[5] In the second half of "Mademoiselle Panache," Lady Augusta ——— and Helen Temple are compared with regard to the distinction between accomplishments and less superficial qualities. Lady Augusta's upbringing has been supervised by the frivolous and unprincipled French governess, Mlle Panache, "while her mother, content with her daughter's progress in external accomplishments, paid no attention to the cultivation of her temper or her understanding."[6] As a result of her education Lady Augusta draws and plays, speaks French and Italian, dances gracefully, and dresses well. But her taste in literature runs to indecent French novels, and her only standard of right and wrong is the behavior of fashionable society. She is a vain and mercenary coquette, who rates her suitors according to their fashion and fortune and cares for none of them. Mrs. Temple, on the other hand, has given her

---

(p. 256, January 24, 1809; p. 259, January 30, 1809), although she has not yet read the work when she refers to it, and also alludes to it in "Catharine" (*Minor Works*, p. 232). She mentions what R. W. Chapman considers to be Miss More's *Practical Piety* (1811) in a letter dated May 31, 1811. (See *Letters*, p. 287, and appendix 5.)

[5] See above note 6, chapter 2.

[6] Maria Edgeworth, *Tales and Novels* (London, 1857), vol. 1: "Mademoiselle Panache" (pt. 2), p. 362. All subsequent references to Maria Edgeworth's works will be to the 1857 edition.

daughters, Helen and Emma, a more solid education, and carefully formed their dispositions. Helen, therefore, although she lacks Lady Augusta's brilliance and polish, has a thinking mind, a feeling heart, and good principles. Lady Augusta and Helen, like Mary Crawford and Fanny Price, become rival candidates for the hand of a young man. Mr. Montague is at first very much taken with Helen; but when he sees Lady Augusta displaying her charms and skill in an archery meet, he transfers his admiration to her. Like Edmund Bertram, he deceives himself into believing that his charming young lady's heart is as amiable as her exterior is engaging:

> A passionate admirer of grace and beauty, he could not help wishing that he might find Lady Augusta's temper and understanding equal to her personal accomplishments. When we are very anxious to discover perfections in any character, we generally succeed, or fancy that we succeed. Mr. Montague quickly discovered many amiable and interesting qualities in this fair lady; and, though he perceived some defects, he excused them to himself with the most philosophic ingenuity. (pp. 382–383)

"Well," he tells himself, "she has time enough before her to learn to think" (p. 379). As he grows to know Lady Augusta better, Mr. Montague is undeceived, and he returns to Helen Temple. Eventually the tutor-companion of one of her beaux so plays upon Lady Augusta's vanity that she elopes with him, and with the elopement the story ends.

Jane Austen herself shows interest in the problem of feminine accomplishments in the unfinished early novel entitled "Catharine," where a motif of contrasting young ladies also appears. Camilla Stanley, in that work, has received a fashionable London education. The reader is told that she

> had been attended by the most capital Masters from the time of her being six years old . . . a period of twelve Years had been dedicated to the acquirement of Accomplishments which were now to be displayed and in a few years entirely neglected. (*Minor Works*, pp. 197–198)

As a result of her upbringing Camilla is elegant and highly accomplished, but she is a thoroughly shallow girl:

> . . . those Years which ought to have been spent in the attainment of useful knowledge and Mental Improvement, had been all bestowed in learning Drawing, Italian, and Music, more especially the latter, and she now united to these Accomplishments, an Understanding unimproved by reading and a Mind totally devoid either of Taste or Judgment. . . . All her Ideas were towards the Elegance of her appearance, the fashion of her dress, and the Admiration she wished them to excite. She professed a love of Books without Reading, was Lively without Wit, and generally good humoured without Merit. (*Minor Works*, p. 198)

Catharine Percival, on the other hand, has been brought up in the country under the strict supervision of her aunt, an admirer of Hannah More's *Coelebs in Search of a Wife.* Although she has not had the instruction in the fine arts and the modern languages that Camilla has had, her aunt's rigorous moral training and her own habit of extensive reading have made Catharine a virtuous and well-informed girl. Camilla and her family come from London to visit Mrs. Percival and her niece, and Catharine is at first much taken with her young relative. Before long, however, she is disenchanted. "She found,"

no variety in [Camilla's] conversation; She received no
Information from her but in fashions, and no Amusement
but in her performance on the Harpsichord; and after
repeated endeavors to find her what she wished, she was
obliged to give up the attempt and to consider it as fruitless.
(*Minor Works*, p. 201)

It should be noted perhaps that Camilla's brother, the
dashing Edward Stanley, who flirts with Catharine without
having serious intentions, bears some resemblance to Henry
Crawford in *Mansfield Park*. Moreover, the talkative, nag-
ging Mrs. Percival somewhat resembles Mrs. Norris. And
there is a naïveté and idealism, sketched with gentle humor,
about Catharine Percival that one also finds in Fanny Price.[7]
It does not seem likely that "Catharine"—or any of the
known juvenilia and fragments—is the prototype of *Mansfield Park*. And there is not, in my opinion, sufficient
biographical information about Jane Austen, or enough
evidence in the works themselves, to make speculation
about the development of the last three novels in their
early stages profitable, as it sometimes has proved to be in
the cases of *Sense and Sensibility* and *Pride and Prejudice*.
It is possible, however, that Jane Austen may have drawn
upon some features of "Catharine" in creating *Mansfield
Park*.[8] At any rate, the subject of feminine accomplishments

[7] Catharine Percival and Fanny Price are otherwise quite different,
however: Catharine lacks Fanny's timidity and possesses a sense of
humor. And "Catharine" and *Mansfield Park* are dissimilar in other
respects: there is, for instance, no apparent equivalent for any member
of the Bertram family in the unfinished novel.

[8] Clearly, I disagree on more than one count with Q. D. Leavis'
theory that the relationship between *Mansfield Park* and *Lady Susan*
is extremely significant. (See Mrs. Leavis' "*Lady Susan* into *Mansfield
Park*," *Scrutiny*, 10 (1941): 114–142.)

is treated in a similar, though not—and this is perhaps important—in the same fashion in both works.

II

Turning to *Mansfield Park*, one should first observe that the distinction between accomplishments and more worthy qualities of mind and heart is used to help define the positions of Fanny Price and Sir Thomas Bertram and most of the members of his family in the moral scheme of the novel. A great deal is said about education and upbringing in *Mansfield Park*, and in looking at the passages on education and its effects in the light of contemporary educational philosophy, one finds that the Bertram girls, with Sir Thomas' full approval, receive precisely the shallow, superficial kind of fashionable education that Hannah More and others opposed. Fanny, under Edmund's tuition, receives an education more in conformity with the *Strictures* —and shows it at every turn.

The Bertram girls and Mrs. Norris present a picture of the educational system that prevails at Mansfield early in the novel when they comment on Fanny's many deficiencies soon after her arrival from Portsmouth. Their indirect description of their schooling tallies almost exactly with the accounts of poor educational programs found in the works of Hannah More and others:

> ... as her cousins found [Fanny] ignorant of many things with which they had been long familiar, they thought her prodigiously stupid, and for the first two or three weeks were continually bringing some fresh report of it into the drawing-room. "Dear Mamma, only think, my cousin cannot tell the principal rivers in Russia—or she never

heard of Asia Minor—or she does not know the difference between water-colours and crayons!—How strange! Did you ever hear any thing so stupid?"

"My dear," their considerate aunt would reply; "it is very bad, but you must not expect every body to be as forward and quick at learning as yourself."

"But, aunt, she is really so very ignorant! . . . I cannot remember the time when I did not know a great deal that she has not the least notion of yet. How long ago it is, aunt, since we used to repeat the chronological order of the kings of England, with the dates of their accession, and the principal events of their reigns!"

"Yes," added the other; "and of the Roman emperors as low as Severus; besides a great deal of the Heathen Mythology, and all the Metals, Semi-Metals, Planets, and distinguished philosophers."

"Very true, indeed, my dears, but you are blessed with wonderful memories, and your poor cousin has probably none at all. . . . And remember that, if you are ever so forward and clever yourselves, you should always be modest; for, much as you know already, there is a great deal more for you to learn."

"Yes, I know there is, till I am seventeen. But I must tell you another thing of Fanny, so odd and so stupid. Do you know, she says she does not want to learn either music or drawing."

"To be sure, my dear, that is very stupid indeed, and shows a great want of genius and emulation. But all things considered, I do not know whether it is not as well that it should be so, for . . . it is not at all necessary that she should be as accomplished as you are;—on the contrary, it is much more desirable that there should be a difference." (pp. 18–19)

As they grew up, the reader is told, "the Miss Bertrams continued to exercise their memories, practise their duets, and grow tall and womanly; and their father saw them becoming in person, manner and accomplishments, everything that could satisfy his anxiety" (p. 20). The Bertram girls' education is an epitome of the errors that Hannah More and others were attacking in Jane Austen's day; and the result of their upbringing is that they are unprincipled, shallow, and unfeeling in the manner of the wrongly educated young ladies of "Mademoiselle Panache" and "Catharine." Each of the girls has "beauty and brilliant acquirements, a manner naturally easy, and carefully formed to general civility and obligingness" (p. 34); but behind their attractive façades there is much that is unlovely. In the absence of any other mental resources, the girls spend their lives in a restless search for amusement—amusement which, in their father's absence, they find in the acting of third-rate, sensationalistic German plays, and in flirting with Henry Crawford. As the *Lovers' Vows* episode shows, they have neither affection for their father nor decency enough to conceal their lack of love and respect. They rejoice in Sir Thomas' dangerous journey—and one should not forget that he *is* "in some degree of constant danger" throughout the trip, being exposed, at a fairly advanced age, to what was considered a perilously unhealthy climate, as well as to two sea voyages. And they take advantage of his absence to indulge in smart, improper frivolity of which they know he would disapprove.[9] Their rivalry over the affections of

[9] It is hardly just to accuse Jane Austen of prudishly turning her back on the theatricals of her own youth in her treatment of the Mansfield production, as some critics have done. She is condemning, not plays and the acting of plays in general, but the state of mind and heart behind the performance of *Lovers' Vows* at Mansfield Park: the indifference to Sir Thomas' danger, the determination to be fashionably, and shallowly, risqué. There seems to me to be little or no evidence to

Henry Crawford reveals the girls' unpleasant lack of either principle or sisterly feeling. The sisters, the reader is told,

> under such a trial as this, had not affection or principle enough to make them merciful or just, to give them honour or compassion. Maria felt her triumph, and pursued her purpose careless of Julia; and Julia could never see Maria distinguished by Henry Crawford, without trusting that it would create jealousy, and bring a public disturbance at last. (p. 163)

The ultimate displays of the girls' real natures are Maria's cold-blooded resolution to marry a rich boor for whom she feels nothing but contempt, and the dual elopement that brings misery and disgrace to their family. Clearly, the Bertram girls' careers are refined parallels to that of Maria Edgeworth's Lady Augusta.

Fanny, not destined by the Bertrams to be a fine lady, never becomes the accomplished woman that her cousins are. She displays at an early age "a fondness for reading, which, properly directed, must be an education in itself" (p. 22), however, and she has her cousin Edmund to stimulate her curiosity, direct her studies, and see that what she reads is, in the words of Hannah More, "grounded in her mind by comment and conversation":

> Kept back as she was by every body else, his single support could not bring her forward, but his attentions were otherwise of the highest importance in assisting the improvement

---

support the theories of some critics that the play is a source for Jane Austen's novel. It is possible, however, that *Lovers' Vows* may have had political implications for Jane Austen's audience, as Avrom Fleishman points out in *A Reading of Mansfield Park* (Minneapolis: University of Minnesota Press, 1967), chap. 3.

of her mind, and extending its pleasures . . . Miss Lee taught her French, and heard her read the daily portion of history; but he recommended the books which charmed her leisure hours, he encouraged her taste, and corrected her judgment; he made reading useful by talking to her of what she read, and heightened its attraction by judicious praise. (p. 22)

Fanny is established as the antitype to the merely accomplished woman. She lacks her cousins' polish, but she possesses "delicacy of taste, of mind, of feeling" (p. 81) and, as Sir Thomas admits at the conclusion of the novel, "the sterling good of principle and temper" (p. 473). She has a taste for literature, and while her cousins are engaged in theatricals and flirtations she reads biography, or poetry, or Lord Macartney's volumes on China in the old schoolroom. And she displays, only too obviously, the "thinking" mind that Hannah More and others were praising as the sign of a cultivated intellect. Some of her remarks, indeed, are painfully, and I believe deliberately, similar to passages from the *Strictures* and similar works. Her speech on memory during her conversation with Mary Crawford in the garden of the Mansfield parsonage is all too clearly an example of the sort of philosophizing on the "secret springs" of the mind that Miss More approves in the remarks on the purposes of the study of history cited earlier:

"How wonderful, how very wonderful, the operations of time and the changes of the human mind! . . . If any one faculty of our nature may be called *more* wonderful than the rest, I do think it is memory. There seems to be something more speakingly uncomprehensible in the powers, the failures, the inequalities of memory, than in any other of our intelligences. The memory is sometimes so retentive, so serviceable, so obedient—at others, so bewildered and so weak—and at others again, so tyrannic, so beyond controul! We are to be sure a miracle every way —but our powers of recollecting and forgetting do seem peculiarly past finding out." (pp. 208–209) [10]

And Fanny's lecture on the evergreen is strikingly, suspiciously, similar to Hannah More's discussion of the "spiry fir" and the "palm tree":

"How beautiful, how welcome, how wonderful the evergreen! When one thinks of it, how astonishing a variety of nature! In some countries we know the tree that sheds its leaf is the variety, but that does not make it less amazing, that the same soil and the same sun should nurture plants differing in the first rule and law of their existence. . . . One cannot fix one's eyes on the commonest natural production without finding food for a rambling fancy." (p. 209)

Very similar to these is the reverie on the stars in which Fanny indulges in chapter 11 of volume 1, a passage discussed later in this chapter. The trouble with all these reflections, of course, is that they sound entirely too much like things borrowed from exemplary educational works; and to this aspect of Fanny's mind I shall also return.

Satisfied that his daughters are acquiring "manner" and accomplishments, Sir Thomas neglects more important aspects of their education; and again because of his worldly bias he is blinded to their real natures. The dual elopement cures Sir Thomas' moral blindness. After the tragedy, he looks back on his girls' education:

He feared that principle, active principle, had been wanting, that they had never been properly taught to govern

10 F. W. Bradbrook (*Jane Austen and Her Predecessors*, pp. 14–15) compares this passage to one in the *Idler*, 74 (September 15, 1759).

their inclinations and tempers, by that sense of duty which can alone suffice. They had been instructed theoretically in their religion, but never required to bring it into daily practice. To be distinguished for elegance and accomplishments—the authorised object of their youth—could have no useful influence that way, no moral effect on the mind. . . .

Bitterly did he deplore a deficiency which now he could scarcely comprehend to have been possible. Wretchedly did he feel, that with all the cost and care of an anxious and expensive education, he had brought up his daughters, without their understanding their first duties, or his being acquainted with their character and temper. (pp. 463–464)

And he welcomes as a daughter the girl whose character has been formed by an education in accordance with the principles of Hannah More.[11]

The theme of education is so prominent in *Mansfield Park* that some critics have believed the novel to be primarily a study of what Fanny Price calls "the effect of education."[12] I do not think *Mansfield Park* is "about" various educational theories and their effects; it is "about" certain mental attitudes, and about types and degrees of moral blindness and moral awareness and their

[11] As Andrew Wright hints in his "A Reply to Mr. Burchell on Jane Austen," *Nineteenth Century Fiction*, 10 (1955): 79–91, it might also be rewarding to consider the relationship between Sir Thomas and Fanny in terms of the relationship between Squire Allworthy and Tom Jones, or the relationships between other father-figures and orphan-figures in eighteenth- and nineteenth-century literature. Jane Austen's treatment of Sir Thomas as an authority figure would seem to be similar to her handling of Mr. Darcy as described in the previous chapter. He is attacked, but also partially vindicated, in the course of Fanny's trip to Portsmouth.

[12] See, for example, Andrew Wright's *Jane Austen's Novels*, p. 22, and R. W. Chapman's *Jane Austen Facts and Problems* (Oxford: The Clark Lectures, 1948), p. 194.

consequences. But the motif of feminine accomplishments, with Sir Thomas as the advocate and Julia and Maria Bertram as the products of an educational system directed toward the acquisition of fashionable accomplishments, helps to define a tendency on the part of Sir Thomas and his family to be overly influenced by the external, the superficial, the social, and to establish Fanny as the representative of more solid and substantial values.

III

Jane Austen's contemporaries would also have seen the distinction between accomplishments and other qualities as a clue to the nature of the relationship of Fanny, Mary Crawford, and Edmund Bertram. Mary is a much-refined version of Maria Edgeworth's or Hannah More's merely accomplished young ladies; Fanny, of their less accomplished but more worthy heroines; and Edmund, of the young men who must choose between the two sorts of women. The love plot does not become a sermon on "the dangers arising from an excessive cultivation of the arts," but it is largely in terms of the problem of the value of accomplishments that the states of mind and heart that move and shape the love plot are gradually revealed.

Thanks to a fashionable London education and the tutelage of her worldly-wise aunt Mrs. Crawford, Mary is a model of social grace and *savoir-faire*. Her dress, her manners—even, as Edmund observes, her "manner of walking" —are flawless. Her musical accomplishments are given particular, deliberate emphasis: like Camilla Stanley, she is an expert musician. After her harp has arrived from London the reader is told that her performance on it "added to her beauty, wit, and good humour, for she played with the greatest obligingness, and there was something clever to be said at the close of every air" (p. 64). Edmund spends his mornings at the parsonage listening to her, and even Fanny is captivated by her playing. Her musical accomplishments play a prominent part in one of the novel's most carefully staged symbolic scenes, the scene in the Mansfield drawing room after dinner in chapter 11 of volume 1.[13] While Fanny lingers at one side of the room, meditating and moralizing on the beauties of a starlit night, in a fashion of which Hannah More would have heartily approved, but which strikes most readers rather less favorably, Mary is displaying her accomplishments in a "glee" at the pianoforte. Edmund is at first stationed at Fanny's side, sharing her feelings, but as the glee progresses she has "the mortification of seeing him advance too, moving forward by gentle degrees towards the instrument, and when it ceased, he was close by the singers, among the most urgent in requesting to hear the glee again" (p. 113). Jane Austen could hardly dramatize the relationship among Mary, Fanny, and Edmund more concisely, or make the fact that she is dealing with an "accomplished woman" and her antitype clearer.

Unlike other writers of the period (the Jane Austen of "Catharine" included), Jane Austen makes her accomplished young lady a truly formidable rival for her heroine. Mary really possesses, and is allowed to display, all of the good qualities that a truly accomplished woman might possess. She has self-assurance, charm, an ability to converse well with all sorts of people. She has, moreover, a quick, witty

---

[13] There is an interesting commentary on the symbolic value of this scene in Henrietta Ten Harmsel's *A Study in Fictional Conventions*, pp. 111–112.

mind. Beside her, with her wit and her liveliness, Fanny Price often appears a social nonentity. But Mary is *merely* accomplished. While doing full justice to all that is attractive in her, Jane Austen sees Mary as a woman who is emotionally and spiritually hollow. She reveals Mary's real nature in one of her subtlest studies in moral blindness—a study that is not sufficiently appreciated by those critics who insist that Mary has a better mind and a warmer heart than Fanny Price. Virginia Woolf, almost alone among modern critics, seems to have observed the subtlety with which Mary's real nature is revealed. Jane Austen, according to Mrs. Woolf, lets Mary

> rattle on against the clergy, or in favour of a baronetage and ten thousand a year with all the ease and spirit possible; but now and again she strikes one note of her own, very quietly, but in perfect tune, and all at once Mary Crawford's chatter, though it continues to amuse, rings flat. Hence the depth, the beauty, the complexity of her scenes.[14]

Mrs. Woolf, however, goes no further in discussing Jane Austen's technique. I heartily agree with her estimate of *Mansfield Park* and Mary Crawford, and I should like at this point to attempt to show that Jane Austen not only intends her readers to see Mary Crawford as a merely accomplished woman, but also succeeds in presenting her convincingly as such—to show some of the ways in which, as it seems to me, Mary's conversation "rings flat."

Her much-discussed wit will serve as a starting-point. Mary is frequently compared to Jane Austen's Elizabeth

[14] Virginia Woolf, *The Common Reader* (London: Hogarth Press, 1925), pp. 177–178. In *The Opposing Self*, pp. 219–220, Lionel Trilling says that Mary's conversation often appears insincere. Mary, he says, "impersonates the woman she thinks she ought to be."

Bennet. Both, it is said, are women of strong feelings and convictions, strongly opposed to hypocrisy, sham, snobbery, convention; and both use their sprightly wit to undermine what they oppose.[15] Thus, in condemning Mary Crawford, Jane Austen is in effect turning her back upon everything that Elizabeth Bennet and *Pride and Prejudice* stand for. This view of Mary's character and her wit is the very reverse of the truth. Elizabeth Bennet's wit is indeed the product of strong feelings and, at times, moral indignation. She ridicules deviations from "what is wise or good" (*Pride and Prejudice*, p. 57)—Darcy's snobbery, Mr. Collins' hypocrisy, Lady Catherine de Bourgh's self-importance—because she cares deeply about goodness and wisdom. Mary's witticisms, in spite of some verbal similarities, prove upon close examination to be humor of a sort that is very different from Elizabeth's. Her wit, at bottom, is the wit of the drawl and the sneer, an almost continual display of smart, rather ugly, sophisticatedness or of shallow cynicism. Far from establishing the two women as kindred

[15] "A way of describing *Mansfield Park* is to say that it is almost the opposite of *Pride and Prejudice*: almost every virtue of freedom, vivacity, and consciousness that is celebrated in *Pride and Prejudice* is condemned in *Mansfield Park*. Mary Crawford of *Mansfield Park* is in every detail of temperament the counterpart of Elizabeth Bennet, the perfection of whose qualities needs no proof, yet Mary Crawford, after having been allowed to charm us, is entirely condemned. . . . *Pride and Prejudice* is militantly anti-snob. It sides with the young against the old. It is anti-religious in its implications, or at least anti-Church. . . . But within the close confines of *Mansfield Park* Jane Austen marshalls every defense of the old way of life against the new." (Lionel Trilling, "A Portrait of Western Man," p. 970.) Compare the opinions of Avrom Fleishman in *A Reading of Mansfield Park*, pp. 16–17 and chap. 3. Marvin Mudrick (*Irony as Defense and Discovery*, p. 169) and Henrietta Ten Harmsel (*A Study in Fictional Conventions*, p. 116) also stress resemblances between Elizabeth and Mary.

spirits, it shows that Mary is, in all essential respects, very nearly Elizabeth's antithesis.

An example is provided by one of the conversations on religion and the clergy for which Mary is sometimes praised. In the course of the Bertrams' and Crawfords' excursion to the Rushworth estate Mrs. Rushworth shows her visitors the family chapel. She notes that although until recent times prayers were read in the chapel twice daily, the late Mr. Rushworth discontinued family prayers. "'Every generation has its improvements,'" Mary remarks to Edmund, "with a smile" and a small debate ensues (pp. 86–88). Fanny is shocked into an enthusiastic defense of the custom of family prayer. "'There is something in a chapel and chaplain so much in character with a great house,'" she says. "'A whole family assembling regularly for the purpose of prayer, is fine!'" Mary replies:

> "Very fine indeed. . . . It must do the heads of the family a great deal of good to force all the poor housemaids and footmen to leave business and pleasure, and say their prayers here twice a day, while they are inventing excuses themselves for staying away."

Edmund points out that "'*that* is hardly Fanny's idea of a family assembling'" and Mary answers:

> "At any rate, it is safer to leave people to their own devices on such subjects. Every body likes to go their own way— to choose their own time and manner of devotion . . . and if the good people who used to kneel and gape in that gallery could have foreseen that the time would ever come when men and women might lie another ten minutes in bed, when they woke with a headach, without danger of reprobation, they would have jumped with joy and envy. Cannot you imagine with what unwilling feelings the former

belles of the house of Rushworth did many a time repair to this chapel? The young Mrs. Eleanors and Mrs. Bridgets—starched up into seeming piety, but with heads full of something very different—especially if the poor chaplain were not worth looking at—and in those days I fancy parsons were very inferior even to what they are now."

Mary shows Elizabeth Bennet's talent for repartee—she thinks quickly, and she expresses herself with a good deal of verbal facility. But the effect that this conversation has, on a second or third reading, is quite different from that produced by one of Elizabeth's sallies. Mary's wit is directed, not at hypocrisy in religion, but at religious practice itself, which she chooses to call an occupation of hypocrites. The humor in the passages just cited consists chiefly in the naughtiness of her original smart impiety; in a smile, from the height of her worldly wisdom, at Fanny's naïveté in believing religious observance to be more than a tedious sham; and in a sneer, from the height of her superiority in fortune, fashion, and appearance, at those dull dogs, the parsons. Is there warmth or concern behind Mary's speeches, or are her "good people," her "belles of the house of Rushworth," the objects of rather contemptuous amusement? Do Mary's remarks resemble Elizabeth Bennet's wit as nearly as they do a sort of humor that, in the following passage, Hannah More (in spite of her unfortunate phraseology) describes in a way that is not without some point? Miss More writes:

> That cold compound of irony, irreligion, selfishness and sneer, which make up what the French ... so well express by the term *persiflage*, has of late years made an incredible progress in blasting the opening buds of piety in young persons of fashion. A cold pleasantry, a temporary cant

word, the jargon of the day . . . blights the first promise of seriousness. The ladies of *ton* have certain watch-words, which may be detected as indications of this spirit. The clergy are spoken of under the contemptuous appellation of *The Parsons*. Some ludicrous association is infallibly combined with every idea of religion. If a warm hearted youth has ventured to name with enthusiasm some eminently pious character, his glowing ardour is extinguished with a laugh; and a drawling declaration, that the person in question is really a mighty *harmless* good creature, is uttered in a tone which leads the youth secretly to vow, that whatever he may be, he will never be a good harmless creature. (*Strictures*, chap. i, p. 315)

Mary's use of the term "parson" ought perhaps to be noted —she is the only character in the novel who does use it—in connection with Hannah More's attack on persiflage. One need not have read eighteenth-century moralists, however, to see the brand of humor in Mary's remarks on the subject of religion for what it is. It is not a very engaging sort of humor; it is certainly not the humor of an Elizabeth Bennet.

The same is true of Mary's other talks on religion. But other samples of her wit bear study too. In a dinner conversation with Edmund and Fanny at Mansfield, Mary describes her difficulties in having her harp transported from Northampton to the Mansfield parsonage:

"I have tidings of my harp at last. I am assured that it is safe at Northampton; and there it has probably been these ten days, in spite of the solemn assurances we have so often received to the contrary. . . . The truth is, that our inquiries were too direct; we sent a servant, we went ourselves: this will not do seventy miles from London—but this morning we heard of it in the right way. It was seen by some farmer, and he told the miller, and the miller told the butcher, and

the butcher's son-in-law left word at the shop . . . I am to
have it to-morrow; but how do you think it is to be con-
veyed? Not by a waggon or cart;—Oh! no, nothing of that
kind could be hired in the village. I might as well have asked
for porters and a hand-barrow. . . . To want a horse and
cart in the country seemed impossible, so I told my maid
to speak for one directly; and as I cannot look out of my
dressing-closet without seeing one farm yard, nor walk in
the shrubbery without passing another, I thought it would
be only ask and have, and was rather grieved that I could
not give the advantage to all. Guess my surprise, when I
found that I had been asking the most unreasonable, most
impossible thing in the world, had offended all the farmers,
all the labourers, all the hay in the parish." (pp. 57–58)

Edmund explains that all the available carts in the neighborhood are needed for carrying in the hay then being harvested,
and Mary replies: "'I shall understand all your ways in time;
but coming down with the true London maxim, that every
thing is to be got with money, I was a little embarrassed
at first by the sturdy independence of your country
customs'" (p. 58). This is a clever, spirited, account; but
one needs to consider the psychology behind it. Mary is not,
as it might seem at first, laughing at herself for her ignorance of country ways; she is displaying her sophistication
by ridiculing the quaint rustics who consider hay more important than harps. Eager dissociation of herself from the
ways of creatures who live "seventy miles from London,"
contempt for farmers, laborers, and hay, a show of her
distaste for farmyards—these are the foundations on which
Mary's wit rests. It is humor of a sort that parades studied
indifference to everything save the appurtenances of met-
ropolitan high life, as it is lived by the likes of Lady

Stornaway and Mrs. Frazer, as a badge of sophistication. The attitudes to which Mary's wit appeals would appear to be considerably closer to those of Miss Bingley than to those of the heroine of *Pride and Prejudice*.

A little later in the course of the same conversation Mary employs her wit again—this time in a nonchalant reference to the mental and moral failings of the admiralty:

> "Of various admirals, I could tell you a great deal; of them and their flags, and the gradations of their pay, and their bickerings and jealousies. But in general, I can assure you that they are all passed over, and all very ill used. Certainly, my home at my uncle's brought me acquainted with a circle of admirals. Of *Rears*, and *Vices*, I saw enough. Now, do not be suspecting me of a pun, I entreat." (p. 60)

Mary delights in suggesting that folly and vice may lurk behind purported wisdom and goodness here as elsewhere throughout *Mansfield Park*. But is the basis of her humor moral concern, or is it, as in the conversation on religion cited earlier, moral *un*concern—flippant, worldly-wise and not very attractive cynicism? Later in the novel she displays her worldly-wise wit in discussing Maria Bertram's indifference to her financé Mr. Rushworth and her flirtation with Henry Crawford:

> ". . . the theatre is engaged of course by those indefatigable rehearsers, Agatha and Frederick. If *they* are not perfect, I *shall* be surprised. By the bye, I looked in upon them five minutes ago, and it happened to be exactly at one of the times when they were trying *not* to embrace, and Mr. Rushworth was with me. I thought he began to look a little queer, so I turned it off as well as I could, by whispering to him, 'we shall have an excellent Agatha, there is something so *maternal* in her manner, so completely *maternal* in

her voice and countenance.' Was not that well done of
me?" (p. 169)

Rushworth's fiancée and the man he has reason to consider
his friend are exposing their deceit and their contempt for
him for all except him to see, and what is Mary's response to
the situation? Is her wit based on indignation, or upon the
acceptance of the ugly business with cynical *sang-froid*?
I must doubt that Elizabeth Bennet's response to the
situation would have been similar.

But it is the cumulative effect of such displays of wit,
rather than any individual passage in the novel, that is most
important. None of the passages just cited, taken by itself,
is likely to impress the reader as overwhelming evidence of
moral depravity on Mary Crawford's part. But time and
again Mary's wit flows in the same channels, almost always
is it based on smart cynicism or supercilious sophisticatedness; and when one has been exposed to it long enough he
begins to sense the presence of an unattractive mind behind
it. Elizabeth Bennet's wit is the wit of a sensitive, impulsive,
sometimes angry young woman. Mary's humor is the
humor of what George Eliot once described as "circles in
which the absence of grave emotion passes for wit." [16]
Mary's nonhumorous conversation also "rings flat"
frequently. In fact, close attention to Mary's conversation
shows, after a while, that the chief difference between her
and the Bertram girls is that Mary manages to conceal the
essential unattractiveness of her mind more successfully
than Julia and Maria do. An overwhelming preoccupation
with money and social position, in· particular, goes

[16] George Eliot, *Daniel Deronda* (New York: Harper & Bros.,
1961), vol. 6, chap. 1, p. 383.

unnoticed, by many readers, because she so often expresses it in a disarming manner.

Mary openly declares that "'every body should marry as soon as they can do it to advantage'" (p. 43). During her disputes with Edmund on the role of fortune and consequence in producing the good life she flattens him with her disconcerting admissions of Philistinism: "'Be honest and poor, by all means—but I shall not envy you; I do not much think I shall even respect you. I have a much greater respect for those who are honest and rich'" (p. 213). And she loudly maintains that "'a large income is the best recipe for happiness I ever heard of'" (p. 213). But of course no one believes her. The reader tends to take her admissions as signs of her impatience with hypocrisy and cant: rather than platitudinize about the unimportance of riches and rank in life, she calls herself a thoroughly mercenary woman. Is this opinion justified, however, or is Mary employing a tactic for self-defense—and self-deceit? The effect that speeches such as Mary's—open, even exaggeratedly worded acknowledgments of unattractive qualities—have, is immediately to lead others—perhaps herself—to doubt them. This phenomenon seems to be at work behind the reader's response to Mary. Like the deluded Edmund Bertram, he tends to look for evidence that Mary's remarks are untrue, and loses sight of the fact that, as such displays of candor often are in life, her admissions are not as far as one might think from representing the speaker's actual state of mind. For if one looks closely at some conversations in which Mary is obviously not speaking for effect, she is found to be expressing similar views in a different form. Mary does in fact believe that a large income is the best recipe for happiness—or at least cannot conceive of a better one. Without realizing it herself, she is continually betraying a snobbish and mercenary mind.

Her first reaction to Fanny, for instance, is an inquiry about Fanny's social position: she "pumps" Edmund and Tom Bertram to find out what Fanny's status in the Mansfield family is, and whether she is "out" (pp. 48–51). When Edmund asks if Mary is acquainted with William Price's captain during the dinner party at Mansfield she replies "with an air of grandeur" that she and her acquaintance "'know very little of the inferior ranks. Post captains may be very good sort of men, but they do not belong to *us*'" (p. 60). The conversation between Fanny and Mary in the garden of the Mansfield parsonage gives an unpleasant picture of Mary's sense of values. Fanny admires the manner in which the little garden in which the girls are sitting has been laid out: "'I must admire the taste Mrs. Grant has shown in all this. There is such a quiet simplicity in the plan of the walk!—not too much attempted'" (p. 209). Mary replies, "carelessly," "'it does very well for a place of this sort. One does not look for extent *here*—and between ourselves, till I came to Mansfield I had not imagined a country parson ever aspired to a shrubbery or any thing of the kind'" (p. 209). Mary's first response to the news that her brother intends to marry Fanny is "'Lucky, lucky girl! . . . what a match for her!'" (p. 291). And although she goes on to felicitate Henry on his choice, she soon reverts to her preoccupation with the social and economic aspects of the match: "'. . . you do not want for fortune; and as to her connections, they are more than good. The Bertrams are undoubtedly some of the first people in this country. She is niece to Sir Thomas Bertram; that will be enough for the world'" (p. 293).

Even Mary's most moving conversation, her last interview with Fanny, reveals similar mental attitudes—and this time there is no question that she is grimly serious about what she is saying. Speaking of her friends Mrs. Frazer and Lady Stornaway, both of whom have made marriages of convenience that have turned out badly, Mary says:

". . . I look upon the Frazers to be about as unhappy as most other married people. And yet it was a most desirable match for Janet at the time. We were all delighted. She could not do otherwise than accept him, for he was rich, and she had nothing; but he turns out to be ill-tempered and *exigeant*; and wants a young woman, a beautiful young woman of five-and-twenty, to be as steady as himself. And my friend does not manage him well; she does not seem to know how to make the best of it. There is a spirit of irritation, which, to say nothing worse, is certainly very ill-bred. In their house I shall call to mind the conjugal manners of Mansfield Parsonage with respect. Even Dr. Grant does shew a thorough confidence in my sister, and a certain consideration for her judgment, which makes one feel there is attachment; but of that, I shall see nothing with the Frazers. . . . Poor Janet has been sadly taken in; and yet there was nothing improper on her side; she did not run into the match inconsiderately, there was no want of foresight. She took three days to consider of his proposals; and during those three days asked the advice of every body connected with her, whose opinion was worth having; and especially applied to my late dear aunt, whose knowledge of the world made her judgment very generally and deservedly looked up to by all the young people of her acquaintance; and she was decidedly in favour of Mr. Frazer. This seems as if nothing were a security for matrimonial comfort! I have not so much to say for my friend Flora, who jilted a very nice young man in the Blues, for the sake of that horrid Lord

Stornaway, who has about as much sense, Fanny, as Mr.
Rushworth, but much worse looking, and with a black-
guard character. I *had* my doubts at the time about her
being right, for he has not even the air of a gentleman."
(p. 361)

In the conversation in which this passage occurs, Mary
comes as close to setting aside her usual habits of mind and
conversation as she is ever to do. She is groping for a vocabulary that will enable her to grasp what has happened during
her stay with Edmund and Fanny. At Mansfield she has,
for the first time, encountered what she can only describe
as "heart":

> "Good, gentle Fanny! when I think of this being the last
> time of seeing you; for I do not know how long—I feel
> it quite impossible to do any thing but love you. . . . I can
> think only of the friends I am leaving; my excellent sister,
> yourself, and the Bertrams in general. You have all so much
> more *heart* among you, than one finds in the world at large.
> You all give me the feeling of being able to trust and confide
> in you; which, in common intercourse, one knows nothing
> of." (p. 359)

And her complacent sophistication is a bit shaken by the
encounter. Yet she cannot quite express—and thus realize—
her suspicion that human relationships can involve something more than self-interest regulated by the laws of
politeness. She can see that much is amiss in London; but
she can think only in terms of errors in judgment and
manners. Marriage is still, to quote one of her earliest conversations, a "'transaction'"; in which one marries for some
"'advantage in the connection, or accomplishment or good
quality in the person'" (p. 46). One trades beauty, fashion,
and accomplishments for rank and fortune and—if one can

get them—good sense and good manners in a husband. She cannot seem to see that the "security"—the word itself is suggestive—that she wonders about must come from a deeper relationship. And herein lies the pathos of Mary's story. She cannot rise far enough above the mental habits of her London set to see them—and herself—as they really are. She is the only major, seriously treated, Austen character who fails to attain a measure of self-knowledge in the course of her story.

Jane Austen once praised her brother Henry's perceptiveness as a judge of Henry Crawford's character. "He admires H. Crawford," she wrote to Cassandra, "I mean properly, as a clever, pleasant man" (*Letters*, p. 378, March 2, 1814). She meant her readers to admire Mary Crawford too, properly, for her vivacity and social graces, but not to lose sight of Mary's essential shallowness. The reader who has observed Mary's conversation closely ought not to be surprised when, after she leaves Mansfield, Mary's attachment to Edmund is "cooled and staggered by a return to London habits," or when her interest in him begins to revive after Tom Bertram becomes seriously ill. Nor is Mary's reaction to the elopement of Maria Rushworth and Henry Crawford inconsistent with her given character. Mary responds to the elopement just as she has responded to almost everything else in the novel, with the attitudes of her smart London set. In speaking of the elopement, as Edmund says, "'She was speaking only, as she had been used to hear others speak, as she imagined every body else would speak'" (p. 456). Publicity, not adultery, concerns her; and she is sure that if Henry and Maria can be maneuvered back into a position of some social respectability, "'married, and properly supported by her own family,'" giving "'good dinners and large parties,'" all will be well. The reader is meant to pity Mary and to regret the fact that a woman who has so many good qualities should lack what is most essential. But to see her as an Elizabeth Bennet, a warm, sensitive woman, a rebel against society's snobbery and conventionalism is to misunderstand badly both her and her author.

Parenthetically, it may be remarked that much of what has been said of Mary applies equally to Henry Crawford. Except for his lack of Mary's strong economic orientation, he is a masculine version of his sister—polished, talented, charming, but essentially shallow. The early signs of his lack of feeling or principle—his cruel flirtations with Maria and Julia Bertram, his plan to captivate Fanny—are obvious enough. But it is sometimes argued that an attachment to a woman like Fanny must make a better person out of a man such as Henry Crawford, and that his elopement with Maria Rushworth is inconsistent with the reformed Henry. Many readers have agreed with R. Brimley Johnson that " 'Henry Crawford *would* have persevered and uprightly' had he been consistently developed." [17] But is there concrete evidence that his love for Fanny works any real change in Henry's character? I think not. It is true that Henry appears to change during his courtship of Fanny. The tone of his conversation changes: he begins to display "sentiment and feeling, and seriousness on serious subjects" (p. 340) in the Mansfield drawing room. And for the first time he takes an interest in his duties as a landlord. But the motives for Henry's behavior are so obviously ambiguous that the conclusion of the novel cannot be called unjustified. Henry energetically discusses religion with Edmund—but only in order to attract Fanny's attention:

> "Our liturgy," observed Crawford, "has beauties, which not even a careless, slovenly style of reading can destroy;

[17] R. Brimley Johnson, *Jane Austen*, p. 143.

but it also has redundancies and repetitions, which require good reading not to be felt. For myself, at least, I confess being not always so attentive as I ought to be—(here was a glance at Fanny) that nineteen times out of twenty I am thinking how such a prayer ought to be read, and longing to have it to read myself—Did you speak?" stepping eagerly to Fanny, and addressing her in a softened voice; and upon her saying, "No," he added, "are you sure you did not speak? I saw your lips move. I fancied you might be going to tell me I *ought* to be more attentive . . . ." (p. 340)

And his new interest in his tenants' welfare, as Jane Austen points out, is "aimed, and well aimed, at Fanny":

". . . it would be simple to be duped by a man who has no right of creditor to dupe me—and worse than simple to let him give me a hard-hearted, griping fellow for a tenant, instead of an honest man to whom I have given half a promise already.—Would it not be worse than simple? Shall I go? Do you advise it?"

"I advise!—you know very well what is right."

"Yes. When you give me your opinion, I always know what is right. Your judgment is my rule of right." (p. 412)

Jane Austen suggests, although the suggestion is not confirmed until the elopement takes place, that there is a suspicious element of artificiality in Henry's presumed change of heart. Henry is consciously playing the role of the reformed rake, as he has played other roles in the past, in order to attract another woman. In his own way, perhaps, he may love Fanny; but his vanity, his desire to attract, is the chief element in his love and the chief motive behind his "reformation." And this same vanity leads him to stay for Mary Crawford's party and to renew his flirtation with Maria Rushworth. Henry might have "persevered, and uprightly," he might even, in time, have been really reformed, have come to love Fanny better than himself, if no temptation had been thrown in the way of his vanity—but that is all that can be said for him.

Just as Sir Thomas' value for his daughters' accomplishments blinds him to their real natures, so Edmund is captivated by Mary's charms to such an extent that he allows himself to be blinded to the Crawfords' shallowness and coldheartedness. And as his attraction toward the "accomplished woman" increases, his ties with her foil are weakened. He brushes aside Fanny's timid but just criticism of the Crawfords. In the manner of Maria Edgeworth's Mr. Montague, he is continually excusing the failings of the woman he so admires. Mary's lapses, he holds, are faults of decorum only, the natural overflowing of high spirits and strong feelings that she has never learned to keep in check: "'she does not think evil, but she speaks it,'" he maintains (p. 269). Even after he has seen her in London he is willing to deceive himself. "I am ready to blame myself for a too harsh construction of a playful manner," he writes to Fanny from London (p. 421). Similarly, he closes his eyes to Henry Crawford's immorality and selfishly glosses over Fanny's dislike for him in his anxiety to promote a match between Fanny and Henry and thus cement the ties between the Mansfield family and the Crawfords. "He is blinded," as Fanny declares in despair.

Mary's changed behavior in London, the elopement of Henry Crawford and Maria Rushworth, and Mary's reaction to the elopement help to bring Edmund back to his senses, and to Fanny. After the elopement he can no longer remain blind to Mary's real nature. "'The charm is broken. My eyes are opened,'" he says to Fanny after the climactic interview with Mary (p. 466): "'I had never understood her before . . . as far as related to mind, it had been the creature of my own imagination, not Miss Crawford, that I had been too apt to dwell on for many months past'" (p. 458). With Edmund, as with Sir Thomas, a deeper appreciation of Fanny's virtues accompanies self-knowledge; and ultimately Edmund comes to return the love that, all along, Fanny has felt for him.[18]

A reading of *Mansfield Park* in terms of the motif of feminine accomplishments, then, suggests that the Crawfords and most of the Bertram family occupy similar positions in the novel's moral scheme. The possession of accomplishments alone, or the attachment of too much value to them, is symptomatic of excessive leanings toward the values of "the world"—of fortune, fashion, elegance, "art"—and this is the spiritual malady that afflicts Mansfield Park and the Crawfords. Fanny's moral position is opposed to both Sir Thomas' and that of the Crawfords, and the same issues are at stake in both the love plot and the plot which concerns the relationship between Fanny and Sir Thomas.

[18] It is interesting to consider Edmund Bertram as a manipulation of the Richardsonian "patrician hero" as well as in his role as the deluded young man who comes to see the worthlessness of mere accomplishments. Edmund obviously bears a strong resemblance to the patrician hero—particularly as he is seen through the eyes of the adoring Fanny. On this point, and the ways in which Jane Austen varies her hero from the stereotype, see Mary Lascelles, *Jane Austen and Her Art*, pp. 66–68, and the relevant chapter in Henrietta Ten Harmsel's *A Study in Fictional Conventions*, especially pp. 111–114. Although Edmund is much more nearly a "straight" Burney-Richardson hero than Mr. Darcy is, he too is ironically treated and shown to have flaws; Fanny's opinions about the perfection of her authority figure have to be altered somewhat.

It remains to examine Fanny and her position a bit more closely.

IV

Much of the criticism of *Mansfield Park* as a morally unattractive work stems from the assumption that Fanny Price represents the novel's ethical norm, and the feeling that Fanny is the prosing, priggish exponent of a frigid, conventional morality. It is certainly true that Fanny has her drawbacks as a heroine. Her excessive mental and constitutional sensitivity, exemplified as they so often are in tears and fears, do her no service with the twentieth-century reader, although Jane Austen's original audience probably responded to them more sympathetically. Her ideas seem annoyingly strait-laced, at times, and she is, at times, a bore. But her ideas do not seem to stem from a frigid conservatism. And, I believe, Jane Austen was probably as much aware of Fanny's really important imperfections as her readers are. Jane Austen did not intend Fanny to be the static "picture of perfection," the moral paragon that many readers take her to be, and resent her for being. She intended Fanny to be seen as a character who, like Sir Thomas and Edmund Bertram, grows painfully into self-knowledge in the course of *Mansfield Park*. Fanny is the spokesman for the opposition to accomplishments and the system of values the novel associates with them. But Fanny's moral vision is not precisely her author's. The quality of many of Fanny's speeches is one indication of this; another is the manner in which Fanny is made to look rather foolish in the course of her trip to Portsmouth to visit her family. Jane Austen treats her antitype to the accomplished person with considerable irony.

It was noted earlier that Fanny's little lectures on memory and on the evergreen sound excessively "bookish." They seem pedantic, out of place in the real-life conversations in which they occur. The same thing can be said of a great deal of Fanny's conversation. For example, there is the speech on the stars that Fanny delivers in the Mansfield drawing room while Mary is displaying her accomplishments:

> "Here's harmony!... Here's repose! Here's what may leave all painting and all music behind, and what poetry only can attempt to describe! Here's what may tranquillize every care, and lift the heart to rapture! When I look out on such a night as this, I feel as if there could be neither wickedness nor sorrow in the world; and there certainly would be less of both if the sublimity of nature were more attended to, and people were carried more out of themselves by contemplating such a scene." (p. 113)

This speech, like the two earlier "lectures," seems derivative. Its reference to the tranquilizing yet elevating effect of the Burkean sublime on a properly receptive soul might have been taken almost verbatim from any one of dozens of textbooks on the picturesque and the sublime.[19] Like the earlier passages it seems too consciously sententious, and its rhetoric of exclamation and asyndeton seems

[19] In "Sources of Jane Austen's Ideas about Nature in *Mansfield Park*," *Notes and Queries*, 206 (1961): 222–224, F. W. Bradbrook compares Fanny's speech to one of the speeches of Emily St. Aubert in *The Mysteries of Udolpho*. Certainly romantic heroines frequently rhapsodize on the beauties of starlit nights in a fashion similar to Fanny's. However, they seldom seem to moralize as explicitly as Fanny does—although their authors often do it for them.

stilted, almost affected, in the context in which the speech occurs. This last feature was also characteristic of the two earlier speeches:

> "How wonderful, how very wonderful the operations of time and the changes of the human mind!... There seems to be something more speakingly incomprehensible in the powers, the failures, the inequalities of memory, than in any other of our intelligences. The memory is sometimes so retentive, so serviceable, so obedient—at others, so bewildered and so weak—and at others again, so tyrannic, so beyond controul!"

> "How beautiful, how welcome, how wonderful the evergreen! When one thinks of it, how astonishing a variety of nature!"

The allusiveness, the sententiousness, the rhetoric of Fanny's speeches cause them frequently to "ring flat," just as cynicism and oversophistication strike false notes in Mary Crawford's conversation.

Why need one assume that Jane Austen, whose severest critics would not deny her an extraordinarily acute sensitivity to language, was unaware of the frequent stiltedness of Fanny's conversation? On the contrary, I believe the unappealing quality of some of Fanny's speeches is deliberate and purposeful. Fanny's conversational deficiencies are meant to be clues to the nature of her moral vision; her morality, as well as her conversation, is "schoolmarmish."[20] If other characters in the novel suffer from oversophistication, overworldliness, Fanny displays the naïvely uncompromising moral vision of one whose education and habits

[20] Margaret Kennedy also comments on the stiltedness of Fanny's language and its possible purposes in her "How Ought a Novelist," *Fortnightly Review*, 172 (1952): 337–344.

have kept her out of touch with social realities: it is not without a certain symbolic appropriateness that her special room at Mansfield Park should be a secluded former school-room, to which she retreats when affairs in the drawing room, the proper milieu of the other women in the novel, become too much for her.[21] Fanny's overstrict notions are not the result of an unbending conservatism such as Jane Austen's Lady Russell, for example, displays. They are the products of a naïve idealism more nearly similar to that of the young Catherine Morland of *Northanger Abbey*. And Fanny's oversimplified moral vision, like that of Catherine, is altered by exposure to the complex world of reality.[22]

[21] For a somewhat different interpretation of the significance of the schoolroom in *Mansfield Park*, see Sister M. Lucy Schneider, C. S. J., "The Little White Attic and the East Room: Their Function in *Mansfield Park*," *Modern Philology*, 63 (1966): 227–235.

[22] Fanny is somewhat similar to Catherine Morland in other ways as well. At times she seems to be a version of the "female Quixote," the young girl whose vision of life is colored by notions derived from romantic literature. Charles Murrah points out the fact that Fanny's "longing for Gothic atmosphere in the Chapel at Southerton" makes her sound very much like the heroine of *Northanger Abbey* ("The Background of *Mansfield Park*," in *From Jane Austen to Joseph Conrad: Essays in Honor of James T. Hillhouse*, eds. Robert C. Rathburn and Martin Steinmann, Jr. [Minneapolis: University of Minnesota Press, 1958], pp. 23–24). Fanny expects the chapel to resemble something from the poetry of Scott, with banners "blown by the night wind of Heaven" and signs that a "Scottish monarch sleeps below" (p. 86). Again, her first reaction to Mr. Rushworth's decision to remove an avenue of trees from the Southerton grounds is "'Does it not make you think of Cowper? "Ye fallen avenues, once more I mourn your fate unmerited"'" (p. 56). See also F. W. Bradbrook (*Jane Austen and Her Predecessors*, pp. 105–108) on the "element of burlesque in Jane Austen's treatment of her heroine," and Avrom Fleishman (*A Reading of Mansfield Park*, pp. 29–35) on Fanny as "the kindred spirit of Marianne Dashwood and other Austen heroines of sensibility."

Fanny, with her exalted, bookish notions of morality, tends to oversimplify the problem of the value of fortune and accomplishments. She wisely realizes that rank, riches, and elegance are not the most important things in life. But she also, rather superciliously, tends drastically to minimize the importance of these things. In fact, she is rather inclined to assume that the absence of riches and refinements is in some way a guarantee of moral superiority, and the only source of true happiness. Affection in a cottage, be it the charming little house that she and William will inhabit as soon as William can make enough money to buy it for her (apparently the idea that William might some day wish to marry never enters her mind), or such approximations as Thornton Lacey or the Price house at Portsmouth, is for her the most admirable form of felicity. She identifies herself with the Prices rather than with the Bertram-Crawford set. Mrs. Price, unlike her sisters, had married for love, "in the common phrase, to disoblige her family"; and Fanny, in defiance of her childhood memories, persists in believing the Price ménage to be a poor but loving family in which affection makes all else unnecessary. In her chagrin at Sir Thomas' attempt to persuade her to make a marriage of convenience with Henry Crawford and at Edmund's attraction to the worldly Mary, she hopes to find consolation in the warm affection of her family. When she thought of her prospective visit,

> ... it seemed as if to be at home again, would heal every pain that had since grown out of the separation. To be in the centre of such a circle, loved by so many, and more loved by all than she had ever been before, to feel affection without fear or restraint, to feel herself the equal of those who surrounded her, to be at peace from all mention of the

Crawfords, safe from every look which could be fancied a reproach on their account! This was a prospect to be dwelt on with a fondness that could be but half acknowledged. (p. 370)

"Manner Fanny did not want" from her family: "Would they but love her, she should be satisfied" (p. 377).

Sir Thomas, however, has a more accurate idea of what the Prices' life at Portsmouth will be than Fanny has. He designs Fanny's trip as "a medicinal project upon his niece's understanding":

> A residence of eight or nine years in the abode of wealth and plenty had a little disordered her powers of comparing and judging. Her father's house would, in all probability, teach her the value of a good income; and he trusted that she would be a wiser and happier woman all her life, for the experiment he had devised. (p. 369)

And although the ultimate object of Sir Thomas' plan—the promotion of a match between Fanny and Henry Crawford —is not realized by the trip, her residence at Portsmouth does make a wiser woman of Fanny. To her dismay she finds that her own family are no more affectionate toward her, or one another, than the Bertram family—and that the Prices are considerably more unpleasant to live with from day to day than the Bertrams are. Her father "scarcely ever noticed her, but to make her the object of a coarse joke" (p. 389). As for her mother:

> Mrs. Price was not unkind—but . . . her daughter never met with greater kindness from her, than on the first day of her arrival. The instinct of nature was soon satisfied, and Mrs. Price's attachment had no other source. Her heart and her

time were already quite full; she had neither leisure nor affection to bestow on Fanny. (p. 389)

Fanny "might scruple to make use of the words,"

> but she must and did feel that her mother was a partial, ill-judging parent, a dawdle, a slattern, who neither taught nor restrained her children, whose house was the scene of mismanagement and discomfort from beginning to end, and who had no talent, no conversation, no affection towards herself; no curiosity to know her better, no desire of her friendship, and no inclination for her company that could lessen her sense of such feelings. (p. 390)

The house is small and noisy; the household affairs are ill-managed: the Price residence "was the abode of noise, disorder and impropriety. Nobody was in their right place, nothing was done as it ought to be" (pp. 388–389). Fanny learns that a small income is not necessarily the best recipe for happiness, and for the first time she begins fully to appreciate the value of "manner," elegance, and money. At Portsmouth,

> she could think of nothing but Mansfield, its beloved inmates, its happy ways. . . . The elegance, propriety, regularity, harmony—and perhaps, above all, the peace and tranquillity of Mansfield, were brought to her remembrance every hour of the day, by the prevalence of every thing opposite to them *here*. . . . At Mansfield, no sounds of contention, no raised voice, no abrupt bursts, no tread of violence was ever heard; all proceeded in a regular course of cheerful orderliness; every body had their due importance; every body's feelings were consulted. If tenderness could ever be supposed wanting, good sense and good breeding supplied its place. (pp. 391–392)

Amid the squalor and vulgarity of Portsmouth, letters from the worldly Mary Crawford, formerly distasteful to Fanny, become a longed-for relief:

> In her present exile from good society, and distance from every thing that had been wont to interest her, a letter from one belonging to the set where her heart lived, written with affection, and some degree of elegance, was thoroughly acceptable. (p. 393)

Even her former *bête noire*, the rakish Henry Crawford, begins to look better to her when his good manners are contrasted with those of the Portsmouth set: ". . . she had never seen him so agreeable—so *near* being agreeable; his behavior to her father could not offend, and there was something particularly kind and proper in the notice he took of Susan. He was decidedly improved" (p. 406). And if the marriage of convenience that Sir Thomas is trying to impose upon her is still repugnant to her, she can see some of the advantages of an economically sound marriage. Were she to marry a man of wealth such as Henry Crawford she might, for instance, be able to remove her sister Susan to infinitely more pleasant and suitable surroundings:

> Poor Susan was very little better fitted for home than her elder sister; and as Fanny grew thoroughly to understand this, she began to feel that when her own release from Portsmouth came, her happiness would have a material drawback in leaving Susan behind. That a girl so capable of being made, every thing good, should be left in such hands, distressed her more and more. Were *she* likely to have a home to invite her to, what a blessing it would be!—And had it been possible for her to return Mr. Crawford's regard, the probability of his being very far from objecting to such a measure, would have been the greatest increase of her

own comforts. She thought he was good-tempered, and could fancy his entering into a plan of that sort, most pleasantly. (p. 419)

At Portsmouth a sadder and wiser Fanny Price renews her allegiance to the "elegance, propriety, regularity, harmony" of Mansfield. "Portsmouth was Portsmouth. Mansfield was home" (p. 431).[23]

Neither Fanny nor Edmund Bertram nor Sir Thomas Bertram is intended to represent *Mansfield Park*'s standard of moral excellence. Nor is Jane Austen, in her treatment of the Crawfords, hypocritically sacrificing all that she admired in her Elizabeth Bennet to a thesis. And if *Mansfield Park* can be said to have a "thesis" at all, it is not a justification of conventionalism; it is an assertion of the fact that both complacent conformity to the standards of "the world" and naïvely idealistic opposition to them require correction by that "most valuable knowledge . . . the knowledge of ourselves." By reading the novel historically, in terms of Jane Austen's treatment of the subject of feminine accomplishments, one can appreciate both the morality and the artistry of *Mansfield Park* better than many modern critics seem to do.

[23] It should be noted perhaps that in the ironic treatment of Fanny just described, Jane Austen is not employing the sort of "definition-by-contrast" that was observed previously in *Northanger Abbey* and *Sense and Sensibility* and that also is used in *Emma*. In criticizing the "bookish" attitudes and behavior of her antitype to the "accomplished" woman, Jane Austen would not have thought of herself as opposing features of her own moral vision to the thinking of authors in the tradition of Hannah More; emphasis on the need to modify such attitudes as Fanny displays would in fact be likely to occur in works in this tradition. Nor are the incidents used to reveal or correct Fanny's deficiencies, inversions or alterations of ones typical of *Mansfield Park*'s fictional analogues. The novel, in spirit, does not seem to differ as dramatically from the works it resembles as many of Jane Austen's other works do.

5

Emma and the "Formula of Romance"

It is clear that an antithesis between judgment and imagination plays an important part in *Emma.* Emma Woodhouse, an "imaginist," as Jane Austen calls her, makes a number of comic but potentially serious errors because of her failure to check her romantic fancy. Mr. Knightley's good judgment is contrasted with Emma's lively fancy, and throughout most of the novel the two are friendly antagonists. Finally, of course, love for Knightley comes to Emma along with the realization of her errors.[1] There is some difference of opinion as to the extent to which Jane Austen allows Knightley's judgment to triumph over Emma's imagination. Some readers feel that *Emma* is primarily an attack—albeit a good-humored one—on Emma Woodhouse and her too lively fancy.[2] Others think that "however many mistakes she makes, the heroine, with her guesses, and imagination

[1] A most perceptive interpretation of the novel in relation to the "imagination-judgment" antithesis is found in F. W. Bradbrook's *Jane Austen: Emma,* E. Arnold's Studies in English Literature, no. 3 (London: E. Arnold, 1961).

[2] See the remarks on *Emma* in Frank O'Connor's "Jane Austen and the Flight from Fancy," *Yale Review,* 45 (1955): 31–47. *Emma,* according to O'Connor, is Jane Austen's "last bold fling at the imagination."

sometimes comes nearer to a full appreciation of the complexity of experience" than Knightley does.[3] And it is certainly true that Emma has the reader's sympathy, and sometimes his admiration, throughout the novel. A great deal of the criticism of *Emma*, in fact, has been concerned with the various ways in which Jane Austen manages to make Emma, in spite of—and sometimes because of—her errors, a thoroughly attractive character.[4]

One important manifestation of the antithesis between imagination and judgment in *Emma* deserves a more thorough investigation than it has yet received. What Mary Lascelles calls the "bookish origin" of the romantic fancies that cause so much trouble for Emma Woodhouse has been noted by several critics. Miss Lascelles remarks that "such a young woman as Emma, so constituted and so circumstanced, could have become acquainted with illegitimacy as an interesting situation, infidelity as a comic incident, only in her reading." [5] And Lionel Trilling has said of Emma that "like Don Quixote and Emma Bovary, her mind is shaped and deceived by fiction." [6] No critic to date, however, has examined the bookish origin of Emma's follies very thoroughly. The parallels between *Emma* and certain other

[3] F. W. Bradbrook, *"Emma,"* p. 50.

[4] In his *"Emma,"* Lionel Trilling deals with this aspect of the novel at some length. Mary Lascelles (*Jane Austen and Her Art*, p. 69) also discusses the reasons for Emma's peculiar charm. And Wayne C. Booth, "Point of View and the Control of Distance in *Emma,"* *Nineteenth Century Fiction*, 16 (1961): 95–116, deals with a major point that is not covered in my discussion. Compare the discussion of *Emma* in Marvin Mudrick's *Irony as Defense and Discovery*, pp. 181–206, and that in E. N. Hughes' *"Emma:* A Dissenting Opinion," *Nineteenth Century Fiction*, 4 (1949): 1–20.

[5] Lascelles, *Jane Austen and Her Art*, p. 69.

[6] Trilling, *"Emma,"* p. 55.

works of the period—particularly romantic novels and satires, such as those of Barrett, George Crabbe, and Charlotte Lennox, on the romantic novel—are, however, striking and important enough to warrant some detailed study. Such a study, in addition to revealing an interesting facet of the imagination-judgment antithesis, provides further confirmation of the view that *Emma* is not simply a condemnation, but also a partial vindication of Emma Woodhouse's romantic imagination. Jane Austen attacks, but also partially vindicates Emma through a complex series of references to what may be called the "formula of romance."

I

Worth a closer look at this point are some of the characteristics of the sort of literature at which the satire of Barrett, Crabbe, and Mrs. Lennox is directed. The standard plot of the eighteenth- and early nineteenth-century romance concerns a character who is either poor, an orphan, of mysterious birth, of low origin, or any one of several combinations thereof, and who falls in love with, and is loved by, a character of higher rank and greater wealth. "Distresses" accumulate, the most frequent causes of distress being parental opposition to the match, the love of unworthy or unattractive men for the heroine—"the determined Perseverance of disagreeable Lovers, and the cruel Persecutions of obstinate Fathers," Jane Austen calls them in "Love and Freindship" (*Minor Works*, p. 77)—and misunderstandings between the lovers themselves. But all of these sources of distress are swept away with incredible ease in the course of the story. The obstinate parent ceases to insist that his child marry another, or he dies. The hero's apparent infidelity is cleared up. The lovers are happily married and blessings are heaped upon them, and often the character who appeared to be of low degree proves to be wealthy and wellborn. If the novelist has a "Gothic" turn of mind the story becomes more melodramatic—the action takes place in ancient castles or ruined abbeys, and ghosts and threats of murder or immurement in dungeons or convents add to the trials of the hero or heroine—but the basic plot is unchanged. The summary above is an adequate description, for example, of both Regina Maria Roche's *The Children of the Abbey* (1798) and Ann Radcliffe's *The Romance of the Forest* (1791), the two romances cited by Harriet Smith in *Emma* (p. 29). The mother of Amanda Fitzallen, the heroine of *The Children of the Abbey*, was the daughter of the Earl of Dunreath. She was disowned by her father when she married Fitzallen, however, and lived in poverty until the time of her death. Unknown to the Fitzallens, the Earl of Dunreath, relenting, has left his estate to Amanda's brother. His will was concealed by Lady Dunreath, the cruel stepmother of Lady Malvina, and the estate passed to Lady Dunreath's daughter. Amanda meets Lord Mortimer, the son of the Earl of Cherbury, and the two fall in love. But Amanda's father is in the employ of the Earl of Cherbury, and fearing that the Earl will be offended by his son's imprudent love affair, he takes Amanda off to Ireland. A long series of misunderstandings and reconciliations ensues. Eventually, however, Amanda discovers the secret of the Earl of Dunreath's will, the Fitzallens are restored to prosperity, and Amanda and Mortimer are married. *The Romance of the Forest* has a more Gothic atmosphere, but the plot is quite similar to that of Mrs. Roche's novel. The uncle of Adeline, the heroine, has murdered her father and succeeded to his title and fortune. Adeline was given to one of the uncle's henchmen and his wife to be brought up as their own child. After she has undergone a series of harrowing adventures, acquired a lover, been abducted by her uncle, and discovered a manuscript written by her dead father in a ruined abbey, the truth about her birth is revealed, and she marries the man of her choice.

The hero of the romantic novel is, of course, a paragon of manly virtue and beauty. But a consideration of the characteristics of the romantic heroine is particularly relevant to a discussion of *Emma*. The heroine is beautiful, and hers is a particular kind of beauty. Almost invariably, she is rather tall and stately. She is delicate, and nature and distress combine to give her a rather pale complexion—an ethereal look was considered more "interesting" than ruddy good health. She must have "fine eyes"—the eyes are the windows of the heart, and expressive ones are a sure indication of sensibility. Thus, the heroine of Mary Robinson's *Vancenza* (179?) is "tall, and finely proportioned."[7] Clarentine, in Sarah Burney's novel of that title (1798), is "tall, light and graceful."[8] Regina Maria Roche describes the heroine of her *Clermont* (1798) as follows:

> She was tall and delicately made; nor was the symmetry of her features inferior to that of her bodily form; but it was not to this symmetry that they owed their most attractive charm . . . it was derived from the fascinating sweetness diffused over them. Her eyes, large, and of the darkest

[7] Mary Robinson, *Vancenza* (London, 1792), vol. 1, chap. 1, p. 17.
[8] Sarah Burney, *Clarentine* (London, 1816), vol. 1, bk. 1, chap. 4, p. 38. Jane Austen read *Clarentine* for the third time in 1807 according to a letter of February 8, 1807 (*Letters*, p. 358).

hazel, ever true to the varying emotions of her soul, languished beneath their long silken lashes with all the softness of sensibility, and sparkled with all the fire of animation; her hair, a rich auburn, added luxuriance to her beauty, and by a natural curl, gave an expression of the greatest innocence to her face; the palest blush of health just tinged her dimpled, fair, and beautifully rounded cheek....[9]

That there was a style of beauty peculiar to romantic heroines was recognized by eighteenth- and early nineteenth-century readers. In Barrett's *The Heroine* (1813) the standard heroine of romance is thus described by the deluded Cherubina:

> A heroine is a young lady, rather taller than usual, and often an orphan; at all events, with the finest eyes in the world. She blushes to the tips of her fingers, and when mere misses would laugh, she faints. Besides, she has tears, sighs, and half-sighs, always ready; can live a month on a mouthful, and is addicted to the pale consumption.[10]

Jane Austen's own Clara Brereton, in *Sanditon*, is "elegantly tall, regularly handsome, with great delicacy of complexion and soft blue eyes," and Charlotte Heywood, when she sees Clara for the first time, thinks her "the most perfect representation of whatever heroine might be most beautiful and bewitching, in all the numerous volumes they had left behind them on Mrs. Whitby's shelves" (*Minor Works*, p. 391).

[9] Regina Maria Roche, *Clermont* (Philadelphia, 1802), vol. 1, chap. 1, p. 7. *Clermont* is one of the Northanger novels.

[10] Eaton Stannard Barrett, *The Heroine* (London: E. Matthews & Marrott, 1927), letter 7, p. 66. All references are to this edition. For Jane Austen's references to *The Heroine* in the *Letters*, see below, note 16.

Even if a heroine grows up in poverty and isolation she manages somehow to become cultivated and elegant. Thus Emmeline, in Charlotte Smith's novel of that title (1788), grows up in a ruined castle with no company but the housekeeper and steward, but manages to become well educated through "uncommon understanding and unwearied application" and to acquire a taste for literature from browsing among the books in the ruined library.[11]

Everything a heroine does or suffers is surrounded by an aura of glamor. If her love betrays her into misconduct—and it seldom does—it is never prosaic or squalid misconduct: she may elope, but she never lies. If the hero appears to be unfaithful, she may sigh or weep, or perhaps feel virtuous indignation, but she is never to be found in an ugly fit of jealousy. (The hero, on the other hand, is rather expected to be jealous.) And her tears fall on the neatly sanded floor of a picturesque rustic cottage, or on the flagstones of a sublime partially ruined castle.

The absurdities of the romantic novel invited satire.[12] In the tale of Ellen Orford in *The Borough* (1810)[13] Crabbe

[11] Charlotte Smith, *Emmeline* (Philadelphia, 1802), vol. 1, chap. 1, pp. 5–9. *Emmeline* is referred to in "The History of England" and in "Catharine" (*Minor Works*, pp. 144, 147, 199). And Mary Lascelles (*Jane Austen and Her Art*, p. 60) suggests that it is the specific object of a considerable amount of parody in *Northanger Abbey*.

[12] In addition to the satires to be discussed, Mary Charlton's *Rosella* (1799) was probably read by Jane Austen and her audience. Maria Edgeworth's short novel "Angelina" (1801) employs a female Quixote of sorts to satirize the novels of the "romantic-revolutionary" school discussed in the following chapter, as does Elizabeth Hamilton's *Memoirs of Modern Philosophers* (1800).

[13] George Crabbe, *The Borough* (London, 1810), vol. 2, letter 20, pp. 123–137. Crabbe, of course, was one of Jane Austen's favorite poets. She mentions reading the preface to *The Borough* in a letter of October 21, 1813 (*Letters*, p. 358).

employs the "mock-heroine" technique that has been mentioned in connection with *Northanger Abbey*.[14] Unlike *Northanger Abbey*, however, the tale of Ellen Orford is bitter tragedy. It is a grimly realistic parallel to the typical romance in almost every detail. Ellen is a poor cottage girl, and she has a love affair with a wealthy young man. But Ellen and her lover are no paragons of virtue, and soon she is pregnant. Instead of apparent infidelity, she is confronted with a lover who tires of her, deserts her, and marries a woman of his own class. And her "distresses" are the sordid economic ones of being discovered to be pregnant, turned out of her stepfather's house, and left to support herself and her child unassisted. Her suffering takes place, not in a romantic cottage owned by clean and charming rustics, but in a hovel which she shares with a "fallen sister," and her child is born an idiot.

There were also various satires of the "female Quixote" type, and as these seem to be particularly relevant to a discussion of *Emma* a brief review of the two most important "female Quixote" novels is in order. The specific targets at which the satire of Charlotte Lennox's *The Female Quixote* (1752) is aimed are heroic romances popular before Jane Austen's time, rather than sentimental and Gothic novels, but the satire is as applicable to *The Romance of the Forest* as it is to *The Grand Cyrus*. Her mother died shortly after Arabella, the heroine, was born. The girl's father is very old, has withdrawn almost completely from society, and leaves Arabella very much to herself. She has grown up on an isolated country estate. She spends most of her time in reading the romances of Scudéry and similar works, and

[14] See chapter 1 on *Northanger Abbey*, note 1, for discussion of the "female Quixote" and "mock-heroine" types of satire.

excessive indulgence in such reading has warped her imagination. Having had almost no worldly experience, she takes her reading literally—every attractive girl is a heroine, and must have a "history" of conquests and adventures:

> Her ideas, from the manner of her life, and the objects around her, had taken a romantic turn; and supposing romances were real pictures of life, from them she drew all her notions and expectations. By them she was taught to believe, that love was the ruling principle of the world; that every other passion was subordinate to this; and that it caused all the happiness and miseries of life. Her glass, which she often consulted, always shewed her a form so extremely lovely, that, not finding herself engaged in such adventures as were common to the heroines in the romances she read, she often complained of the insensibility of mankind, upon whom her charms seemed to have so little influence.[15]

She even comes to speak in the stilted language of her favorite heroines. Arabella's romantic notions involve her in predicaments both embarrassing and dangerous. She is continually imagining that the most unlikely people—a gardener whom she suspects of being a nobleman in disguise, her aging uncle—are violently in love with her, and she is equally adroit in providing imaginary lovers for her young cousin, Miss Glanville. Her notions make her a prey to designing fortune hunters, one such schemer almost succeeding in gaining her hand and fortune by pretending that he is a prince in disguise and that he is dying for love of her.

[15] Charlotte Lennox, *The Female Quixote* (London, 1799), vol. 1, bk. 1, chap. 1, pp. 7–8. Jane Austen read this work twice and declared, in a letter of January 7, 1807, that she enjoyed it more on the second reading than she had on the first (*Letters*, p. 173).

In spite of her romantic excesses, however, Arabella has many good qualities. She is intelligent, and, when she is not pursuing her *idée fixe*—and occasionally even when she is— a brilliant conversationalist. Her loving, unselfish disposition is shown in her devotion to her sickly father. And although we know her Quixotism is folly, there is an element of magnanimity about her notions that contrasts very favorably with the petty selfishness and vanity of the London belle, Miss Glanville. Fortunately Arabella's sensible but not very romantic cousin, Mr. Glanville, is really in love with her, patiently sees her through her romantic follies, and ultimately marries her.

Jane Austen read Barrett's *The Heroine* (1813) in March, 1814, when *Emma* was in its early stages.[16] *The Heroine* is in many respects quite similar to *The Female Quixote*. Cherry Wilkinson, the "heroine," is the daughter of a prosperous farmer. Her mother is dead, and the girl has been brought up in the country, with almost no companions but her father and a governess. This governess has had a bad influence upon her charge. Cherry is naturally imaginative, and instead of working to correct this propensity, her teacher has inflamed her imagination by allowing her to read works such as *The Children of the Abbey* and the novels of Mrs. Radcliffe. At the time when the story begins, the governess has just left Cherry. The girl begins her "heroic" career by imagining that she is the orphan daughter of a nobleman and that her father is a villain employed by a wicked relative to conceal her from the world. Her mission in life, she decides, is to uncover the mystery of her birth and prove herself to be wealthy and wellborn. A series of

[16] She pronounced it to be "a delightful burlesque, particularly on the Radcliffe style" in a letter of March 2, 1814 (*Letters*, pp. 376–377).

"adventures" follows. Cherry, now self-styled Cherubina de Willoughby, runs away to London, where an impoverished actor impersonates a hero in romance, hoping to persuade her to marry him, and another villain plans to seduce her by taking advantage of her *idées fixes*. Cherubina, like Arabella, has a patient and sensible lover, Robert Stuart, who remonstrates with her on her follies and rescues her from dangerous situations. Gradually, without quite realizing it until the end of the book, Cherubina comes to return his love. Talks with a wise clergyman and a reading of *Don Quixote* lead her to see the error of her ways.

Cherubina, like Arabella, is an appealing character in spite of her follies. There is an exuberance and vitality about her that is extremely engaging. Her wit and ingenuity almost make her an interesting character in her own right, apart from her role as a burlesque heroine. She loves her father deeply: her feeling for him nearly causes her to see though the illusory "history" that she has invented about him on several occasions. She is compassionate—and even practical—in her treatment of the poor: one of the best scenes in the book occurs when Cherubina, in the approved heroic fashion, lodges at the house of a family of peasants—and then winds up cooking and scrubbing for them. Again, her heroic visions have a breadth of scope about them that the reader rather admires when they are contrasted to the pettiness of the life around her. Cherubina herself says:

> Have not all persons their favourite pursuits, and do not all brave fatigue, vexation, and calumny, for the purpose of accomplishing them? One woman aspires to be a beauty, another a title, a third a bel esprit; and in effecting these objects, health is sacrificed, reputation tainted, and peace of mind destroyed. Now my ambition is to be a Heroine . . .

have I not far greater merit, in getting a husband by sentiment, adventure, and melancholy, than by dressing,
gadding, dancing, and singing? (Letter 1, p. 30)

And the reader is rather inclined to agree with her.

The female Quixotes that Jane Austen knew, then, share
the beliefs that love is "the ruling principle of the world"
and that ultimately the course of true love will run smooth.
Every hero or heroine is sure of being irresistibly charming
to one or more lovers. Inequalities of fortune or condition
are no obstacles to romance, and at any rate will probably
be done away with before the end of the history. In addition,
our two heroines have certain similarities in situation and
character in common. Both grow up under conditions which
tend to foster, rather than to repress, their bad propensities.
They live in retirement and are deprived of the watchful
care that an alert parent or a suitable governess could provide. Both make fools of themselves, and are made fools of
by schemers, because of their romantic beliefs. Both have
true lovers, whom they eventually marry. And both, in
spite of their mistaken notions, are warmhearted, vital
characters, free from petty vanity and selfishness.

II

One part of *Emma* that is quite clearly related to romances
and satires of romance is the story of Jane Fairfax. If *Emma*
is viewed in the light of the romances and satires of Jane
Austen's day, it might appear at first that Jane's story would
be perfectly at home in a romantic novel. Jane, a penniless
orphan, becomes involved in a love affair with the wealthy,
well-connected Frank Churchill. There is a domineering
parent, Mrs. Churchill, in the background to oppose the
match; there is distress—for Jane, at any rate—and there is

a serious misunderstanding between the lovers. Like others of the sisterhood of heroines Jane has managed to become remarkably cultivated and elegant in spite of her background. And she even looks a great deal like a heroine, as Jane Austen shows in the most detailed bit of personal description she ever produced:

> Her height was pretty, just such as everybody would think tall, and nobody could think very tall; her figure particularly graceful; her size a most becoming medium, between fat and thin, though a slight appearance of ill-health seemed to point out the likeliest evil of the two. Emma could not but feel all this; and, then, her face—her features—there was more beauty in them all together than she had remembered; it was not regular, but it was very pleasing beauty. Her eyes, a deep grey, with dark eye-lashes and eye-brows, had never been denied their praise; but the skin, which she had been used to cavil at, as wanting colour, had a clearness and delicacy which really needed no fuller bloom. It was a style of beauty, of which elegance was the reigning character. . . . (p. 167)

Jane, tall, elegant, with fine eyes and a pale complexion, pining away from frustrated love and lack of nourishment— she eats so little for breakfast that she must resort to baked apples in the middle of the day, her aunt reports—is in some ways the "perfect representation" of a romantic heroine. Jane Austen takes some pains to stress Jane Fairfax's resemblance to conventional heroines in person and in situation. She does so, however, in order that certain marked differences between Jane and the Amandas and Adelines of fiction may emerge with marked clarity.

For while the matter of Jane Fairfax's story might have come from a romantic novel, the manner in which Jane Austen treats the story is realistic and ironic. In some respects the story is similar to Crabbe's burlesque of the romantic novel, a presentation of a "romantic" tale as it would be if it occurred in real life. Jane Austen shows us that the "formula of romance"—poor but worthy and attractive orphan plus eligible lover—does not always produce the same results in life that it brings about in novels. Jane Fairfax is no impeccable heroine who feels none but the most delicate emotions, behaves with the utmost propriety, suffers under the most delectable conditions, and is rewarded with a paragon among men and unqualified matrimonial bliss. Under the pressures of frustrated love and parental disapproval she consents to a clandestine engagement and a continual practice of dishonesty—a "system of hypocrisy and deceit," as Emma calls it—which she knows to be wrong and which will be a source of shame to her for the rest of her life. The consequence of the engagement, Jane says to Mrs Weston, has been for her

> "a state of perpetual suffering . . . and so it ought. But after all the punishment that misconduct can bring, it is still not the less misconduct. Pain is no expiation. I can never be blameless. I have been acting contrary to all my sense of right; and the fortunate turn that everything has taken, and the kindness I am now receiving, is what my conscience tells me ought not to be." (p. 419)

Her unhappy love affair reduces Jane to a pallid bundle of nerves, in the approved romantic fashion. But Jane does not suffer in a romantic cottage or ruined castle; she pines in the shabby gentility of the Bates' crowded apartment, with her aunt's prattle continually in her ears. Small wonder that in her distress she deviates from the pattern of exemplary and "interesting" heroines and becomes "captious and irritable to a degree that must have been—that was—hard for [Frank] to bear" (p. 419). Small wonder that she becomes most unheroically jealous of Frank's attentions to Emma. Nor is Jane rewarded with unalloyed happiness at the conclusion of her history. Frank and a fortune are hers, but there is still the consciousness of her own misconduct. And she has been painfully made aware that her husband-to-be is no hero, that in many ways he is very much the selfish, spoiled child of good fortune that Mr. Knightley takes him for—a man who will ride to London to personally select a pianoforte and music for her, but who is so pleased with his own ingenuity in creating a "front" of a preference for Emma Woodhouse that he will not cease his attentions to Emma even when he knows that he is causing his fiancée pain. Jane Austen does not utterly demolish the formula of romance, in the way that Crabbe does, but she alters its operations and results significantly.

The story of Jane Fairfax, however, is only one element in a larger pattern of comments on romance that permeates all of *Emma*. The histories of Emma Woodhouse and Harriet Smith must also be considered. While Jane Fairfax is in part a mock heroine, Emma herself is markedly similar to the female Quixotes of Jane Austen's contemporaries. She is not, as far as the reader knows, a devotee of romantic fiction—she never admits to having read anything more compromising than Mme de Genilis' *Adelaide and Theodore* (1783) an "educational" novel (p. 461). She does not speak in the flowery, inflated language, the "thorough novel slang" as Jane Austen calls it (*Letters*, p. 404, September 23, 1814), that heroines of romance and their antitypes in satire employ. But a close look at *Emma* reveals that it is a "female Quixote" novel from which the crude device of novel-reading, as the sole cause of the heroine's absurdities, has been removed. Emma is an "imaginist" by nature. She grows up under conditions that tend to foster her imaginative propensities. She lives in a small country town, and sees little of the world. Her father, like Arabella's, is old and a recluse. He is no companion for his daughter. Early in the novel the reader is told that Emma is "in great danger of suffering from intellectual solitude" after Miss Taylor has left her:

> She dearly loved her father, but he was no companion for her. He could not meet her in conversation, rational or playful.
> The evil of the actual disparity in their ages (and Mr. Woodhouse had not married early) was much increased by his constitution and habits; for having been a valetudinarian all his life, without activity of mind or body, he was a much older man in ways than in years . . . . (p. 7)

Emma's governess, if she does not inflame her imagination with novels, at least provides little intellectual discipline for her:

> Even before Miss Taylor had ceased to hold the nominal office of governess, the mildness of her temper had hardly allowed her to impose any restraint; and the shadow of authority being now long passed away, they had been living together as friend and friend very mutually attached, and Emma doing just what she liked; highly esteeming Miss Taylor's judgment, but directed chiefly by her own. (p. 5)

Just as Arabella has her Mr. Glanville, and Cherubina her Robert Stuart, Emma has Mr. Knightley standing by to censure her follies and eventually to marry her. And where the female Quixotes are the prey of deceitful young men who play up to their romantic notions, Emma is imposed upon by the romantic role-playing of Frank Churchill.

Almost all readers of her story are struck by the fact that Emma is a very attractive character in spite of all of her follies, and much of the criticism of *Emma* has dealt with the means Jane Austen employs to make such a wrong headed girl so very engaging. Some of her most attractive characteristics might be traced back to her sister Quixotes. Like Arabella and Cherubina, Emma is witty and intelligent, and has a sort of intellectual vitality that is appealing. And there is a magnanimity, a lack of pettiness and selfishness in some of her actions of which there are rudimentary traces in Arabella and Cherubina. When she is confronted with Mr. Elton's proposal, for instance, her primary thought is of Harriet, and not of her own humiliation:

> It was a wretched business, indeed!—Such an overthrow of every thing she had been wishing for! Such a blow for Harriet!—That was the worst of all. Every part of it brought pain and humiliation, of some sort or another; but, compared with the evil to Harriet, all was light; and she would gladly have submitted to feel yet more mistaken—more in error—more disgraced by mis-judgment, than she actually was, could the effects of her blunders have been confined to herself. (p. 134)

Some of her best qualities are expressed in terms of the filial love and the compassion for the unfortunate that were found in the other female Quixotes. Emma is a loving and self-sacrificing daughter—and moreover, she sacrifices without self-pity, or even self-congratulation. What seems merely a bow to conventional conceptions of filial love in Arabella and Cherubina becomes a credible and endearing emotion in Emma. The reader can believe that when she thought of leaving her father to marry Mr. Knightley she "wept over the idea of it, as a sin of thought" (p. 435), because he has seen her, throughout the novel, indefatigable in promoting his happiness in every respect, great or small, and patient in bearing with his imbecility. Emma can forget herself—and even, like Cherubina, her customary romanticism—in dealing with people in real distress, as shown in the scene in which she and Harriet visit a poor family in the village:

> She understood their ways, could allow for their ignorance and their temptations, had no romantic expectations of extraordinary virtue from those, for whom education had done so little; entered into their troubles with ready sympathy, and always gave her assistance with as much intelligence as good will . . . she quitted the cottage with such an impression of the scene as made her say to Harriet, as they walked away,
> "These are the sights, Harriet, to do one good. How trifling they make every thing else appear!—I feel now as if I could think of nothing but these poor creatures all the rest of the day; and yet, who can say how soon it may vanish from my mind?" . . .
> "And really, I do not think the impression will soon be over . . . I do not think it will," stopping to look once more at all the outward wretchedness of the place, and recal the still greater within. (pp. 86–87)

The characteristics that have just been reviewed would suggest, to an early nineteenth-century reader, that he view Emma and her career in the light of the "female Quixote" novels of Barrett and Charlotte Lennox. But more important, and more obvious, is the fact that Emma, although she may not be a novel reader, operates on the female Quixote's assumptions about the power of love and the smoothness of its course. She does not—and, as Mary Lascelles has pointed out, this is another thing which makes her appealing in spite of her follies—apply her notions to herself.[17] She exercises her Quixotism on behalf of others, notably Harriet Smith.

Actually, Harriet is a mock heroine of the humorous sort, similar in some respects to Catherine Morland. She is merely a pretty, good-humored, ignorant girl, the antithesis of the heroine Emma tries to make of her. In appearance she is the very reverse of the heroic type, being "short, plump and fair, with a fine bloom, blue eyes, light hair, regular features, and a look of great sweetness" (p. 23). Emma, significantly, resolves "to throw in a little improvement to the figure, to give a little more height, and considerably more elegance," and to "doctor" her eyebrows and eyelashes when she paints her protégée's picture. There is a mystery about Harriet's birth—but her father proves to be a bourgeois of moderate wealth. Her charms prove to be far from irresistible: three men who by all the laws of romance should have been madly in love with her remain immune to her attractions. It is part of Jane Austen's irony that Emma's disordered imagination should select Harriet for the heroine's role in her imaginary histories, while failing to notice the more obvious heroineship of Jane Fairfax.

For Emma, pleased with Harriet's looks and manners, and intrigued by her lack of visible connections, does her best to turn her protégée into a heroine of romance. She applies the romantic formula, beautiful orphan plus eligible young man, to Harriet and a series of suitors, real and imaginary. Robert Martin, who is in fact a catch considerably

[17] Mary Lascelles, *Jane Austen and Her Art*, p. 69.

beyond the expectations of a girl in Harriet's position, is rejected: he is not rich or refined enough to play the hero's role in Emma's history. Mr. Elton fits the formula, and Emma in bold defiance of prudence, probability, and Mr. Elton's observed propensities, decides that he must love and marry Harriet. Mr. Knightley, playing "judgment" to Emma's "imagination," sums up the real situation of Harriet and Mr. Elton with his customary bluntness:

> "What are Harriet Smith's claims, either of birth, nature or education, to any connection higher than Robert Martin? She is the natural daughter of nobody knows whom, with probably no settled provision at all, and certainly no respectable relations. She is known only as a parlour-boarder at a common school. She is not a sensible girl, nor a girl of any information. She has been taught nothing useful, and is too young and too simple to have acquired any thing herself. At her age she can have no experience, and with her little wit, is not very likely ever to have any that can avail her. She is pretty, and she is good tempered, and that is all." (p. 61)
>
> "Depend upon it, Elton will not do. Elton is a very good sort of man, and a very respectable vicar of Highbury, but not at all likely to make an imprudent match. He knows the value of a good income as well as anybody. Elton may talk sentimentally, but he will act rationally. He is as well acquainted with his own claims, as you can be with Harriet's." (p. 66)

But practical matters and probability are no obstacles to Emma. She counters with the female Quixote's belief in the power of love:

> [Mr. Knightley] . . . might have heard Mr. Elton speak with more unreserve than she had ever done, and Mr. Elton

might not be of an imprudent, inconsiderate disposition as to money-matters; he might naturally be rather attentive than otherwise to them; but then, Mr. Knightley did not make due allowance for the influence of a strong passion at war with all interested motives. Mr. Knightley saw no such passion, and of course thought nothing of its effects; but she saw too much of it, to feel a doubt of its overcoming any hesitations that a reasonable prudence might originally suggest; and more than a reasonable, becoming degree of prudence, she was very sure did not belong to Mr. Elton. (pp. 67–68)

And in her blindness she even imagines for Harriet the age-old climax to a romantic history, the discovery that she is wellborn and wealthy. " 'There can be scarcely a doubt that her father is a gentleman—and a gentleman of fortune—' " she says to Mr. Knightley. " 'That she is a gentleman's daughter, is indubitable to me; that she associates with gentlemen's daughters, no one, I apprehend, will deny.— She is superior to Mr. Robert Martin' " (p. 62). Mr. Elton, of course, declines to play Mortimer to Harriet's Amanda, and Emma is silenced for a while. But it is not long before she is envisioning an even more spectacular match between Harriet and Frank Churchill, oblivious to the ever increasing signs of an attachment between Frank and Jane Fairfax that Knightley begins to notice.

Emma's snobbery and her managerial tendencies have been the subject of a great deal of critical comment.[18] These unattractive qualities, as well as her matchmaking, can be explained in terms of her tendency to "fictionalize"

[18] By Edgar F. Shannon, for instance, "*Emma*: Character and Construction," *PMLA*, 71 (1956): 637–650. Lionel Trilling mentions Emma's snobbery in his "*Emma*."

the real world around her. For Emma's Quixotism is not confined to attempts to make the romantic affairs of Harriet Smith work out with the perfection of fiction. Consistently, she deals with the life around her as if it were the material for an impossibly heightened and perfect "history." In the manner of romance, the prosaic and the vulgar elements of Highbury are carefully excluded from Emma's history. The Coxes are dismissed from existence with a few sharp words. The Coles are preserved from oblivion only in order that they may give a party at which all of Emma's favorite characters can assemble. Miss Bates and her dullness she avoids whenever she can. And like a bad novelist, Emma will deal only with characters whom she can easily handle. The select little coterie with which she surrounds herself, with the important exception of Mr. Knightley, is composed of characters whom she can—or thinks she can—arrange in perfect order in her imaginary volume. Miss Taylor is docile and yielding, Harriet Smith will think whatever Emma leads her to think, and Mr. Woodhouse is an intellectual invalid. Mr. Elton and Frank Churchill are Emma's intellectual inferiors, and she believes that she can manage their affairs as she pleases. Jane Fairfax, whose character and intellect are too strong for her to be very malleable material, is banished to a peripheral position in the history—charged with having a love affair with her best friend's fiancé and dismissed to a life of privation and penance as a governess. (Knightley, the novel's realist, tries to force Emma to accept the prosaic Miss Bates and her "unmanageable" niece, just as he tries to force her to accept Robert Martin as a suitor for Harriet.) Mrs. Elton is quadruply repellent as a very vulgar woman, the symbol of Elton's refusal to play the role Emma designed for him, a creator of illusory histories of her own, and a determined, if ineffectual, manager of characters in her own right. Emma cannot exclude Mrs. Elton from her consciousness as easily as she can dismiss the Coxes, but she does her best.

Finally, one should note the additional role that Mrs. Elton plays in *Emma*'s pattern of references to romance. Her resemblance to Emma in her attempt to manage Jane Fairfax's life just as Emma has made a protégée of Harriet Smith has been noted frequently.[19] (The important difference between Emma and Mrs. Elton with respect to their "managing" is that Emma is motivated partly by her vain belief in her own abilities, and partly by genuine benevolence, while Mrs. Elton patronizes Jane Fairfax only in order to gratify her own sense of self-importance.) Another respect in which Mrs. Elton constitutes a vulgar parallel to Emma is in her creation of a romantic "history" about her own courtship and marriage. In reality, of course, she married for an establishment and Elton was motivated by pique and economics. But Mrs. Elton represents herself as a heroine willing to sacrifice the delights of Maple Grove for love, and Elton as a frantic, despairing lover. Her conversation—unlike Emma's—is permeated with "novel slang." Like a true "heroine," she delights in inappropriate lines of poetry, references to "Hymen's saffron robe," and other false elegancies; even her favorite "*caro sposo*" is borrowed from

[19] By James Gregory Murray, "Measure and Balance in Jane Austen's *Emma*," *College English*, 16 (1954): 160–166; by Mark Schorer, "The Humiliation of Emma Woodhouse," *The Literary Review*, 2 (1958): 547–563; by Wayne C. Booth, "Point of View and the Control of Distance in *Emma*"; by Howard Babb in *The Fabric of Dialogue*, p. 183; by Laurence Lerner in *The Truthtellers: Jane Austen, George Eliot, D. H. Lawrence* (New York: Schocken Books, 1967), pp. 100–101.

her reading: critics have noted its appearance in *Cecilia*, and in Jane West's *Letters to a Young Lady*,[20] and it is also to be found in Frances Brooke's *Lady Julia Mandeville* (London, 1763), 1: 68.[21]

Clearly, then, in *Emma* Jane Austen is borrowing heavily and obviously from various kinds of satires on romance readers and writers. Emma Woodhouse is a much-refined female Quixote who employs a substitute in the form of a comic mock heroine to carry out her adventures and who, ironically, is unaware until the conclusion of the story of the far from delicate distresses undergone by a mock heroine of another sort in her vicinity; meanwhile a disagreeable parallel to the chief female Quixote is provided in Mrs. Elton.[22] And Emma's female Quixotism and the other

[20] See E. E. Duncan-Jones, "Notes on Jane Austen," p. 15, and F. W. Bradbrook, *Jane Austen and Her Predecessors*, p. 49; Bradbrook (p. 117) also comments on the expression "Hymen's saffron robe."

[21] Mr. Elton's language is also derivative and artificial, most notably, perhaps, in what we hear of his proposal to Emma (pp. 129–131). It is interesting to note, too, that his expression "woman, lovely woman," which occurs at the climax of his charade—an expression to which Mr. Woodhouse, appropriately, calls attention by repeating it with approbation—was a resounding cliché of the day. It probably had its origin in a speech by Jaffeir in *Venice Preserved* (Act I, sc. 1, line 335), and was picked up by the novelists. "Woman—lovely woman! thou hast charmed me, though, perhaps, it would not be easy to find one to whom my reason would allow me to be constant," declares the hero of Mary Wollstonecraft's *Mary: A Fiction* (London, 1788), 16: 94. "Woman, lovely woman, then, alone, has been my bane," says a character in *Isabinda of Bellefield* ("By Mrs. Courtney" [Dublin, n. d.], 33: 118). The phrase was apparently recognized by Dickens as a cliché of bygone days, for he puts it into the mouth of the old beau Mr. Turveydrop in *Bleak House* who uses it with "very disagreeable gallantry" to Esther Summerson. (*The Works of Charles Dickens* [London: Thomas Nelson & Sons, 1904], vol. 10, chap. 14, p. 205.)

[22] Edward M. White notes several of the similarities between *Emma* and parodies of romance in his "*Emma* and the Parodic Point of View,"

mock-romantic elements in the novel helped to define for the early nineteenth-century reader the nature of Emma's mental dilemma—her propensity to let her imagination run away with her judgment, to expect reality to conform to the demands of her romantic imagination.

Emma's excessive indulgence in her "bookish" romantic notions leads her to moral blindness, makes her insensitive, unjust, and occasionally unkind to the real people around her. She cannot appreciate Robert Martin, or his love for Harriet, because he is not a hero in appearance or manner. She overestimates—with potentially grave results for Harriet—her protégée's worth, merely because Harriet is pretty and her situation is interesting. She decides that Jane Fairfax is a reprehensible character largely because Jane resists with a stubborn reserve all attempts to be managed. (See especially pp. 168–169, where the degree of Jane's guilt changes from moment to moment according to the degree of favor Jane is in.) She misunderstands everyone's feelings. She imagines Harriet to be in love with Frank Churchill when Harriet has set her cap for Mr. Knightley. She decides that Jane Fairfax is in love with Mr. Dixon when Jane loves Frank Churchill. She imagines that Frank is in love with herself, when Frank loves Jane. And she fails to perceive her own abiding love for Mr. Knightley until (as she thinks) she is in danger of losing him.

What Emma needs, and gets in the course of the novel, are several generous doses of self-knowledge, the perception of her own limitations of vision, and of the causes of them. The realization that she has been wrong in believing that Mr.

Nineteenth Century Fiction, 18 (1963): 55–63. White reaches, by a different route, conclusions similar to my own about the attitude toward "romance" and "reality" embodied in *Emma*.

Elton was in love with Harriet is one stage in her development. "She had taken up the idea . . . and made every thing bend to it," she admits (p. 134). She resolves never to take an active part in matchmaking again, and, following the interview in which she has to tell Harriet the truth about Mr. Elton, the reader is told that "she left [Harriet] with every previous resolution confirmed of being humble and discreet, and repressing imagination all the rest of her life" (p. 142). The lecture Knightley delivers after Emma has been rude to Miss Bates at Box Hill perhaps marks another stage in her development; it makes her resolve to be more tolerant of the prosing but worthy old woman. But it is the series of revelations which occurs toward the end of the novel that causes her really to see herself as she is. After Harriet has revealed her affection for Mr. Knightley, following the news of Frank Churchill's engagement to Jane Fairfax, and Emma has realized that "Mr. Knightley must marry no one but herself," she confesses in a moment of painful self-awareness to her blindness and to the folly of attempting to arrange the lives of real people as if they were "characters" to be manipulated at will:

> Every moment brought a fresh surprise; and every surprise must be matter of humiliation to her.—How to understand it all! How to understand the deceptions she had been thus practising on herself, and living under!— The blunders, the blindness of her own head and heart! (pp. 411–412)

> With insufferable vanity had she believed herself in the secret of everybody's feelings; with unpardonable arrogance proposed to arrange everybody's destiny. She was proved to have been universally mistaken; and she had not quite done nothing—for she had done mischief. (pp. 412–413)

"'I seem to have been doomed to blindness,'" she admits to Mr. Knightley at the beginning of the conversation that is to rescue her from despair (p. 425).[Perceptiveness follows a realization of her faults,] and soon Emma can appreciate Robert Martin, see that Harriet belongs with him, and be a sympathetic friend to Jane Fairfax.[And, having attained the maturity that is the goal of the Austen heroine, Emma is rewarded with a happy marriage.]

III

But Jane Austen does not condemn Emma's "visions of romance" entirely. One of the ways in which she defines her more complex attitude toward Emma is through a further manipulation of the materials of romance and antiromance. Mary Lascelles has commented on the fact that the "female Quixote" novels present a picture of reality that is in its own way as unsatisfactory as that presented in the novels that they satirize:

> For, while they condemn the proffered flattery of the novelists as insincere, they accept it at the novelists' own valuation: perceiving (that is) that those writers aim at presenting a rose-coloured view of life, they uncritically assume that the world they show is prettier than actuality. Consequently, the discovery of the actual world is, for their heroines, a dull, sad process of disenchantment, hardly eased by the perfunctory reflection that reality may have some pleasures of its own.[23]

What these satires do, in effect—and the same thing may be said with equal justice of the satire of Crabbe—is to imply that "reality" is the opposite of "romance," to create an

[23] Mary Lascelles, *Jane Austen and Her Art*, p. 71.

antithesis between romance and reality, between the worlds of imagination and reason. Jane Austen, with her customary refusal to accept life as a matter of black and white, does away with this antithesis by presenting the reader, and the enlightened Emma, with a reality that, while it does not always conform to the standards of romance, nevertheless includes within itself an imaginatively satisfying element of romance. This concept of reality is made evident in the novel's series of love affairs, each of which is related to the romantic formula. The series, viewed in the light of the romance-reality, "imagination-judgment" antithesis that Jane Austen encourages her reader to keep in mind, becomes a commentary on the nature of reality, and a partial vindication of Emma's romantic imagination.

In the first place there is the story of Jane Fairfax and Frank Churchill. In their story Jane Austen undermines the formula of romance considerably. But, as was suggested earlier, she by no means accepts the sordid concept of reality presented by a satirist such as Crabbe. What she does is to strike a mean between the "romance" of Mrs. Radcliffe or Charlotte Smith and the "reality" of Crabbe. Where the romantic heroine experiences a series of delicate distresses, and Ellen Orford becomes pregnant, Jane Fairfax is forced into a clandestine engagement. Where the romantic hero appears to be unfaithful, and the heroine sheds a few graceful and dignified tears, where Ellen's lover deserts her to marry a woman of his own station and leaves her in squalid economic distress, Frank Churchill inconsiderately flirts with Emma Woodhouse, and Jane is jealous and hurt. Where the romantic heroine's lover turns out to be a paragon of virtue and leads her to a life of happiness ever after, and Ellen's young man is a cad who leaves her to eternal misery, Jane is left in a state of qualified happiness with a rather spoiled young man. Ultimately, in Jane Austen's hands, the romantic formula is partially successful—it works with a number of qualifications, but it nevertheless works.

In addition to the story of Jane Fairfax, there is the marriage of Harriet Smith to Robert Martin. And Miss Taylor, whose situation in life almost exactly parallels that of Jane Fairfax, loves and marries Mr. Weston. The Taylor-Weston match is a real-life love affair—Mr. Weston is hardly a romantic hero—which nevertheless follows the formula of romance. Miss Taylor, the poor but attractive, accomplished, and deserving governess—she is also an orphan, apparently, for one never hears of relatives—wins the heart of the comfortably wealthy owner of Randalls. Whatever obstacles there may have been to the match are easily swept away by Emma. (When Emma tells Mr. Knightley that if she had not "'smoothed many little matters, it might not have come to any thing at all'" and says that he "'must know Hartfield enough to comprehend that'" [p. 13] she is presumably referring to Mr. Woodhouse's aversion to matrimony and unwillingness to part with those to whom he has grown accustomed: Mr. Woodhouse, as the nominal head of the family in which Miss Taylor is a dependent, appears to be humorously cast in a sort of "objecting parent" role with regard to the match.) And there is the traditional heaping up of blessings at the conclusion of Miss Taylor's romance: she is comfortably settled within walking distance of her closest friends, she is on excellent terms with her son-in-law, and she is expecting a child.

It is the success of Miss Taylor's match that encourages Emma to apply the formula of romance in the Harriet-Elton affair. Here, of course, she is frustrated and forced to see that the formula does not always apply to real life. The Harriet-Knightley affair does something more. For not only does the formula not work here, but the reader—and Emma—breathe a sigh of relief at finding that it does not work. One is made to see that there may be circumstances in which, if love were to conquer all, the result would be anything but fortunate. For there is a vast gap between Harriet and Mr. Knightley, not merely in birth and fortune, but in intellect and general habits of mind. For a man of Knightley's nature to marry a girl such as Harriet—a girl whom he himself has called merely good-tempered and ignorant—would be a tragically imprudent step, one likely to result in a marriage like that of Mr. and Mrs. Bennet or that of Sir Thomas and Lady Bertram. At the conclusion of the novel, however—when Emma is wise enough to realize it—Harriet does make a match which, if it does not quite conform to the extravagant demands of romance, is nevertheless beyond her reasonable expectations.[24]

Jane Austen thus carries on a rather complex definition of reality in terms of the formula of romance. Reality, for her and the enlightened Emma, is a place where romance is not as prevalent as one might think—or as romantic; or as desirable. But reality is not the antithesis of romance. Jane Fairfax achieves a tolerable degree of happiness after her

[24] Compare R. E. Hughes, "The Education of Emma Woodhouse," *Nineteenth Century Fiction*, 16 (1961): 69–74. Hughes points out the importance of the love and marriage pattern, but interprets it in a way that differs from my interpretation. According to Hughes, Emma's education is double. First, she must recognize the importance of socioeconomic factors in marriage. The Harriet-Elton affair makes her aware of these factors. Then she begins to keep social and economic factors uppermost in her mind. But the nonprudential romance between Jane Fairfax and Frank Churchill helps to give her a more well-balanced point of view.

months of pain. Harriet Smith, although she is rejected by the mercenary Elton, is loved by a man above her station. For the blessed few, the Miss Taylors and Mr. Westons, reality is nearly as perfect as the romantic imagination could wish. And as a conclusion to the story of her female Quixote's disillusionment, Jane Austen has reality obligingly approach the perfection of fiction once more. Emma falls truly and deeply in love with Knightley at last. She finds herself in the romantic novelists' favorite situation, torn between love and filial duty. But the objections of that stern parent, Mr. Woodhouse, to his daughter's marriage are miraculously removed by the hand of fate (or is it the hand of Mr. Weston?); and she and Knightley are married:

> ". . . really it is strange; it is out of the common course that what is so evidently, so palpably desirable—what courts the pre-arrangement of other people, should so immediately shape itself into the proper form. . . . There does seem to be a something in the air of Hartfield which gives love exactly the right direction, and sends it into the very channel where it ought to flow.
>
> The course of true love never did run smooth—
>
> A Hartfield edition of Shakespeare would have a long note on that passage." (pp. 74–75)

It would have to be a very long note indeed—as long as a novel, perhaps. For, to Jane Austen, if romance is not reality, reality is never altogether unromantic. If an "imaginist's" demand for an unreasonable degree of romantic perfection in life may make her, and those around her, unhappy, nevertheless cool judgment alone has no monopoly on the truth.

6

Persuasion and "Modern Philosophy"

How eloquent could Anne Elliot have been,—how eloquent at least, were her wishes on the side of early warm attachment and a cheerful confidence in futurity, against that over-anxious caution which seems to insult exertion and distrust Providence!—She had been forced into prudence in her youth, she learned romance, as she grew older—the natural sequel of an unnatural beginning. (p. 30)

Persuasion is often considered Jane Austen's capitulation to "romance." Many critics have felt that after stressing in earlier novels the need for a qualification of "sensibility" by "sense," of imagination by judgment, of "nature" by "art," Jane Austen "learned romance," and in her last complete work produced a novel that constitutes a moral about-face from her earlier views.[1] Lady Russell's prudence and

[1] Thus Virginia Woolf (*The Common Reader*, p. 204) feels that in *Persuasion* Jane Austen "is beginning to discover that the world is larger, more mysterious, and more romantic than she had supposed. We feel it to be true of herself when she says of Anne: 'She had been forced into prudence in her youth, she learned romance as she grew older—the natural sequel of an unnatural beginning.'" R. Brimley Johnson (*Jane Austen*, pp. 149–150) believes that "at the door of death, whether or not she saw it opening to receive her, Jane Austen

the elegance and sophistication of the Bath circle are rejected, and Captain Wentworth and his naval colleagues, as the embodiment of warmheartedness and "romance," triumph. Anne Elliot's youthful prudence almost causes her to become an unhappy old maid. Fortunately, however, Anne repents and escapes from a world of heartless elegance to one where love and friendship prevail. This interpretation is open to question, however, for the quotation at the beginning of this chapter does not tell the whole story of *Persuasion.*

Clearly the novel does dramatize a conflict of values that can be classified under the headings of "prudence" and "romance," "sense" and "sensibility," "art" and "nature." The characters in the story are grouped into "sets" on the basis of the distinctions between "art" and "nature." The Bath set, consisting of Sir Walter Elliot and his daughter Elizabeth, William Elliot, Lady Dalrymple and Miss Carteret, Colonel Wallis and, with certain important reservations, Lady Russell, is associated with "art." "Nature" is represented by the set composed of the "navy" characters, the Crofts, Harvilles, Benwick and Wentworth, and of the family from Uppercross. Mary Elliot Musgrove, with her coldheartedness and snobbery, acts as a foil to the "worth and warmth" of the characters by whom she is

deliberately, clearly, and emphatically prefers the dashing impetuosity, the manly charm and impulsive wooing of a Wentworth, over the pleasing and courteous eloquence of an Elliot, the motherly wisdom of a Lady Russell." Frank O'Connor, in "Jane Austen and the Flight from Fancy," calls *Persuasion* "the revenge of [Jane Austen's] imagination on her judgment." And W. R. Martin, "Sensibility and Sense: A Reading of *Persuasion,*" *English Studies in Africa,* 3 (1960): 119–130, states that *Persuasion* "stands *Sense and Sensibility* on its head": prudence, as embodied in Lady Russell, is attacked, and sensibility, represented by Anne, Wentworth and the "navy" characters, triumphs.

surrounded, a piece of the Elliot world transposed to the world of Uppercross and Lyme. The two sets of characters are clearly distinguished, and often specific points of contrast between them are emphasized explicitly. "Nature"— the countryside around Uppercross and the picturesque natural setting of Lyme—is the proper milieu of the Upper-cross-navy set. The Musgroves and their nautical friends take long walks to admire the beauties of the countryside and investigate the picturesque scenery of the seacoast at Lyme. The Bath characters thrive in the cosmopolitan atmosphere of the busy, populous resort. Similarly, with the exception of Wentworth and, possibly, Benwick, the Uppercross-navy characters tend to be, like Mr. and Mrs. Musgrove, "friendly and hospitable, not much educated, and not at all elegant." They are rough diamonds, whose warmth and gregariousness are contrasted with the Bath group's demand for sophistication and elegance. A large, noisy Christmas party is the Musgroves' delight, but Lady Russell quits the scene of their Christmas celebrations in disgust, preferring the hubbub of the streets of Bath to the revelry of the Musgrove and Harville children. At Lyme the Harvilles are "almost hurt" because Wentworth will not bring the entire party from Uppercross to dine with them, in spite of the fact that their house is "so small as none but those who invite from the heart could think capable of accommodating so many." At Bath, Elizabeth Elliot will not invite her own relatives to dinner because she does not think she has enough servants to carry off the performance with elegance. In the Uppercross-Lyme world marriages are made for love; the Bath characters marry for money or for social position. Fanny Harville is permitted to engage herself to Captain Benwick under circumstances that are almost exactly the same as those which caused the Elliots and Lady Russell to disapprove of Anne's engagement to Wentworth. The Musgroves' willingness to assist their daughters to make, if not imprudent, at least not advantageous marriages for love is contrasted with the Elliots' refusal to make things easier for Anne.[2]

It is also true that Lady Russell, the principal representative of the Bath set, proves to have been a bad counselor for Anne. Lady Russell's brand of "prudence" is undesirable, and she and Anne both learn that it is—Anne has learned the lesson before the story begins; Lady Russell is to see the error of her ways before it closes. But does Anne react

---

[2] In "Structure and Idea in Jane Austen's *Persuasion*," *Nineteenth Century Fiction*, 8 (1953): 272–279, Joseph M. Duffy stresses social differences between the "navy" characters and the Elliot circle that seem to be worth consideration. "The decline of the hereditary landed aristocracy and the ascendency of the energetic naval class," as represented by the Crofts' renting of Kellynch Hall, is an important element in the novel, he feels. And the reconciliation between Wentworth and Lady Russell is "a compromise between the most loved representative of the aristocracy and the most loved representative of the Navy." Although R. W. Chapman has attacked the idea that there was anything like a class distinction between the Elliots and the "navy" characters in his "A Reply to Mr. Duffy on *Persuasion*," *Nineteenth Century Fiction*, 9 (1954): 154, reminding us that Sir Walter was not a member of the aristocracy and that the naval officer in Jane Austen's day was usually the younger son of a peer, a country gentleman or a clergyman, there seems to be a great deal of truth in Duffy's interpretation. The point Jane Austen apparently stresses is that Wentworth and his circle are self-made men who have risen from comparative poverty through their own efforts, while the Elliots and their friends are proud of resting on their ancestors' laurels. Certainly, too, Sir Walter feels that there is a marked social distinction between himself and the naval officers in the novel; he objects to the navy because it is "'the means of bringing persons of obscure birth into undue distinction, and raising men to honours which their fathers and grandfathers never dreamt of'" (*Persuasion*, p. 19).

against the dictates of prudence instilled in her in her youth by giving an unqualified assent to "romance"? Is Wentworth, the chief representative of the navy set, the moral center of the novel? The first thing that should cause questioning of such an interpretation is the fact that, even though Anne realizes that Lady Russell's advice was wrong, she maintains resolutely throughout the novel that she was right, at the age of nineteen, in taking it and breaking her engagement. At the beginning of the novel, in the paragraph which precedes the one with which this chapter began, one reads that Anne "at seven and twenty, thought very differently from what she had been made to think at nineteen" on the subject of the broken engagement: "She did not blame Lady Russell, she did not blame herself for being guided by her" (p. 29). In her last conversation with Wentworth she is still maintaining that she was right—and Wentworth is admitting that it is he who was wrong in resenting her breach of the engagement. Moreover, if *Persuasion* is read in terms of the opinions of Jane Austen's contemporaries on the issues that the broken engagement raised for them, Anne Elliot is even less likely to appear as a convert to "romance" who renounces "prudence." Indeed, she emerges as the moral ideal of the novel. And *Persuasion* itself appears not as Jane Austen's capitulation to "romance" but as a reconciliation of "art" and "nature" very much in the Austen tradition.

I

When Anne defends her action in breaking the engagement toward the close of *Persuasion*, her chief line of defense is that it was her duty to sacrifice her inclinations in deference to the woman who had been "almost a mother" to her. "'I have been thinking over the past,'" she says,

"and trying impartially to judge of the right and wrong, I mean with regard to myself; and I must believe that I was right, much as I suffered from it, that I was perfectly right in being guided by the friend whom you will love better than you do now. To me, she was in the place of a parent. Do not mistake me, however. I am not saying that she did not err in her advice. It was, perhaps, one of those cases in which advice is good or bad only as the event decides; and for myself, I certainly never should, in any circumstances of tolerable similarity, give such advice. But I mean, that I was right in submitting to her, and that if I had done otherwise, I should have suffered more in continuing the engagement than I did even in giving it up, because I should have suffered in my conscience. I have now, as far as such a sentiment is allowable in human nature, nothing to reproach myself with; and if I mistake not, a strong sense of duty is no bad part of a woman's portion." (p. 246)

At the end of the novel, of course, Wentworth is all complaisance. But, like Othello, he is not receptive to the analogy between marital and filial duty until late in his career. Before he and Anne are reconciled he can see Anne's breaking the engagement only as a sign of deplorable weakness on her part. In order to appreciate the full significance of Anne's adherence to filial duty, and Wentworth's belief that Anne's deference to Lady Russell cannot be defended, one must turn to the literature of Jane Austen's day.

The title of *Persuasion*, like those of "Love and Freindship," *Sense and Sensibility*, and *Pride and Prejudice*, is an expression borrowed from the language of eighteenth- and early nineteenth-century novelists and moralists, and it calls attention to one of the novel's major issues.[3] The term "persuasion" was used in a rather specialized sense in Jane Austen's day. Conflict between a parent who wishes his child to make a marriage that is socially and economically acceptable and a child who wants to follow the inclination of his heart seems to be an eternally interesting subject; it was particularly appealing to the writers and readers of Jane Austen's period. Case histories of the sad results of parental despotism or filial imprudence in affairs of the heart abound in the novels and appear in many of the other literary forms of the period. And a parental attempt to influence a child's choice of a matrimonial partner was frequently described as "persuasion." In *Sir Charles Grandison*, for instance, the term is often used in connection with the matrimonial controversy between Lady Clementina and her parents. Speaking of Lady Clementina's plight Harriet Byron says to Mr. Lowther, "'. . . persuasion, Sir, in the circumstances this lady is in, is compulsion'" (vol. 7, letter 15, p. 88). Sir Charles tells Harriet that he would not have Lady Clementina "'either compelled, or over-earnestly persuaded'" by her parents (vol. 7, letter 15, p. 92). Lady Clementina justifies her flight to England by saying:

> ". . . determined as I was against entering into a state I too much honour to enter into it with a reluctant heart, *could* I take any other step than that I have taken, to free myself from the *cruelty* of *persuasion?*" (vol. 7, letter 27, p. 134).

[3] There is no conclusive proof that Jane Austen herself chose the title for *Persuasion*, as R. W. Chapman points out in his "Jane Austen's Titles," *Nineteenth Century Fiction*, 9 (1954): 238. Jane Austen's literary executors, however, would have been as familiar with the term and its applications in the literature of the day as she was.

Mrs. Williams, the exemplary mother in Jane West's *The Advantages of Education* (1793), bewails having, in her not-so-exemplary youth, "yielded to the persuasions of those around me" and married a man she did not love for his money.[4] The term is used in Charlotte Smith's *Emmeline* (1788), when Emmeline's uncle tries to force her into marrying a wealthy old man. Lady Augusta Montreville, Emmeline's cousin, writes: "I have heard . . . that no endeavours will be omitted to drive you to marry Rochely; and that they will persecute you every way, both by persuasions, and by distressing you."[5] In the lengthy moral summary at the end of her *The Mysterious Warning* (1796), Mrs. Parsons reviews the careers of various characters and concludes that:

> A parent has an undoubted right to a negative voice, to *persuade*, to *reason*, and *direct* a young and inexperienced mind; but to force a child to the altar, from motives of ambition, interest, or to gratify any selfish passions, too generally lays the foundations for that indifference, and neglect of the domestic duties, which terminates in folly, vice, and the ruin of all social happiness.[6]

The "persuasion" theme, the theme of love versus filial duty and social propriety, was fascinating to Jane Austen's contemporaries. To most of them the idea of filial obedience had an almost mystical appeal that was due partly to its relation to the Christian virtue of humility, partly to the fifth

---

[4] Jane West, *The Advantages of Education*, vol. 2, chap. 9, p. 113.

[5] Charlotte Smith, *Emmeline*, vol. 1, chap. 19, p. 215.

[6] Eliza Parsons, *The Mysterious Warning* (London, 1796), vol. 4, chap. 10, pp. 264–265. See note 3 to chapter 1 for Jane Austen's references to Mrs. Parsons.

commandment, and partly, probably, to age-old sentiments and beliefs about the analogy between paternal, regal, and divine authority in a divinely ordered world.[7] The sanctity of love was not to be denied, however; hence the fascination of the problem. The majority of Jane Austen's contemporaries were agreed as to what seemed a feasible solution to the problem of the clash between love and filial duty. They clung to the time-honored tradition that a child should give up a match of which his parents disapproved, but need not marry against his own inclinations in order to please his parents. Thus the exemplary heroine of Mary Brunton's *Self-Control* (1810), like Eliza Parsons, was "firmly of the opinion that parental authority extended no farther than a negative voice."[8] And in his *Enquiry into the Duties of the Female Sex* (1797), Thomas Gisbourne states that "although parental authority can never be justified in constraining a daughter to marry against her will, there are many cases, in which it may be justified in requiring her to pause."[9]

But traditional views on love, duty, and social propriety were being challenged at the turn of the eighteenth century. The chief challengers were the writers of the romantic-revolutionary school who declared themselves disciples of

[7] See chapter 3 of J. M. S. Tompkins' *The Popular Novel in England*, and chapter 12 of Margaret Dalziel's *Popular Fiction 100 Years Ago* (London: Cohen & West, 1957) for interesting discussions of the significance of the theme of filial piety in the eighteenth century and the early Victorian period.

[8] Mary Brunton, *Self-Control* (Edinburgh, 1811), vol. 2, chap. 15, p. 309. Jane Austen mentions *Self-Control* three times in the *Letters*: on April 30, 1811 (p. 278); on October 11, 1813 (p. 344); and in November or December, 1814 (p. 423). She has not yet read it in 1811; she is reading it for the second time in 1813.

[9] Thomas Gisbourne, *An Enquiry into the Duties of the Female Sex*, 11: 177.

Rousseau and Godwin.[10] Godwin opposed unreasonable submission to any of society's traditions and beliefs. "There is but one power," he wrote in *Political Justice* (1793), "to which I can yield a heart-felt obedience, the decision of my own understanding, the dictate of my own conscience. The decrees of any other power, especially if I have a firm and independent mind, I shall obey with reluctance and aversion."[11] He praised the firm, independent, "energetic" character, the man or woman possessed of "fortitude" enough to defy social pressures and traditional systems of authority and follow the convictions of his reason:

> Instead of fortitude, we are carefully imbued with maxims of artifice and cunning, misnamed prudence. . . . when shall we arrive at the land of realities, where men shall be known for what they are, by energy of thought, and intrepidity of action! It is fortitude, that must render a man superior alike to caresses and threats, enable him to derive his happiness from within, and accustom him to be, upon all occasions, prompt to assist and to inform. Every thing therefore favorable to fortitude, must be of inestimable value. . . .[12]

Rousseau had asserted the right of the irresistible impulses of a noble heart, as well as the convictions of a superior understanding, to take precedence over archaic conceptions of duty, honor, and propriety. The romantic-revolutionary

[10] I am indebted to chapter 8 of J. M. S. Tompkins' *The Popular Novel in England* and to chapter 6 of A. B. Shepperson's *The Novel in Motley* (Cambridge, Mass.: Harvard University Press, 1956), in my discussion of the romantic-revolutionary novelists and their critics.

[11] William Godwin, *Political Justice* (London, 1798), vol. 1, bk. 3, chap. 3, p. 212. Describing a gentleman of her acquaintance in a letter of May 21, 1801, Jane Austen wrote, "*He* is as raffish in his appearance as I would wish every Disciple of Godwin to be" (*Letters*, p. 133).

[12] Godwin, *Political Justice*, vol. 2, bk. 6, chap. 6, p. 280.

novelists tended to combine the ideas of *Political Justice* and Rousseau's political writings with an emphasis, in the manner of the *Nouvelle Héloise*, on passion and sensibility. The peculiar blend of passion and political theory that is characteristic of their works is well illustrated by Mary Hays's *Memoirs of Emma Courtney* (1796).

For Emma, the heroine of the *Memoirs*, ardent passions are the greatest glory of man. "Rousseau was right," she declares, quoting the *Nouvelle Héloise*, "when he asserted that 'common men know nothing of violent sorrows, nor do great passions ever break out in weak minds. Energy of sentiment is the characteristic of a noble soul.'"[13] On the other hand, there are long digressions in which marriage, organized religion, and the subjugation of women are condemned. Emma's history is the story of a grand passion frustrated by society's conventions. She falls madly in love with a young man, Augustus Harley, who is secretly married. With devastating rationality she declares her love for him in defiance of convention, and when he remains unreceptive to her advances even offers to live with him out of wedlock. At length she marries another man, but they are miserable together, and her lack of affection for him is ultimately responsible for his death. Emma is willing to admit that she would have been happier if she had been able to regulate her passions. But her irrepressible emotions, the signs of her superior mental abilities, are far from being a source of shame to her. "What are passions," she declares,

> but another name for powers? The mind capable of receiving the most forcible impressions is the sublimely im-

[13] Mary Hays, *Memoirs of Emma Courtney* (New York, 1802), vol. 2, chap. 15, p. 95. All references will be to this edition.

provable mind!! . . . the vulgar stupidly wonder at the
effects of powers, to them wholly inconceivable: the weak
and the timid, easily discouraged, are induced, by the first
failure, to relinquish their pursuits . . . but the bold and the
persevering, from repeated disappointment, derive only
new ardour and activity. (vol. 1, chap. 15, p. 95)

In a more enlightened social order, she feels, she would not
have been condemned to a life of frustration and disappointment by archaic prejudices and institutions. Her memoirs
end on a note of optimism. Enlightened thinking, promoted
by men and women who have the fortitude to stand above
conventional conceptions of honor and duty, will at length
prevail, and in the future men and women will be able to
follow their hearts and consciences without restraint.
"Hitherto there seems to have been something strangely
wrong in the constitutions of society"; yet,

> men begin to think and reason; reformation dawns, though
> the advance is tardy. Moral martyrdom may possibly be the
> fate of those who press forward, yet, their generous efforts
> will not be lost.—Posterity will plant the olive and the
> laurel, and consecrate their mingled branches to the memory
> of such, who, daring to trace, to their springs, errors the
> most hoary, and prejudices the most venerated, emanci-
> pate the human mind from the trammels of superstition,
> and teach it, *that its true dignity and virtue, consists in being
> free.* (vol. 2, conclusion, p. 158)

In the romantic-revolutionary novel parental interference
with the love affairs of their children becomes a symbol of
the restraint which society's laws and traditions place on the
sensitive, intelligent individual, and unwillingness or in-
ability to submit to parental prerogative becomes the sign
of a courageous, enlightened spirit. In her *Mary: A Fiction*

(1788), for instance, Mary Wollstonecraft added condemnation of parental prerogative and social conformity to the tale of a frustrated grand passion. Mary is the only surviving child of a pair of coldhearted aristocrats. When she is only seventeen her parents marry her to a boy whom she has never met until the ceremony takes place. The marriage is not consummated: immediately after the ceremony her boy-husband goes off on a tour of the Continent. Her parents die, and Mary accompanies a sick friend to Lisbon, where she meets a man to whom she is greatly attracted. Under the influence of her regard for him Mary becomes more and more conscious of her parents' cruelty in forcing her into a loveless marriage: "Her cheeks flushed with indignation, so strongly did she feel an emotion of contempt at having been thrown away—given in with an estate."[14] She is soon deeply in love. Her friend dies and, faced with the prospect of returning to England and consummating her sham marriage, Mary rebels: "Could she set a seal to a hasty vow, and tell a deliberate lie; promise to love one man, when the image of another was ever present to her—her soul revolted" (16: 99). When the time comes for her to leave Lisbon, she resolves to follow her heart. Her parents were not justified in imposing a marriage on her. The marriage is not morally binding. She will defy society's conventions and forsake her husband. "Every cause in nature," she declares, "produces an effect";

> and am I an exception to the general rule? Have I desires implanted in me only to make me miserable . . . can I conform to the maxims of wordly wisdom? can I listen to the cold dictates of worldly prudence, and bid my tumultuous

[14] Mary Wollstonecraft, *Mary: A Fiction* (London, 1788), vol. 13, p. 76. All references will be to this edition.

passions cease to vex me, be still, find content in grovelling pursuits, and the admiration of the misjudging crowd, when it is only one I wish to please—one who could be all the world to me ... I am bound by human ties; but did my spirit ever promise to love, or could I consider when forced to bind myself—to take a vow, that at the awful day of judgment I must give an account of. My conscience does not smite me, and that Being who is greater than the internal monitor, may approve of what the world condemns; sensible that in Him I live, could I brave His presence, or hope in solitude to find peace, if I acted contrary to conviction ... what could the world give to compensate for my own esteem? (18: 109–111)

Mary's lover, however, dies, and she joins her husband. She devotes herself to various philanthropic enterprises and pines away, a victim of parental prerogative.[15]

Conservative novelists and moralists reacted to the romantic-revolutionary writers' iconoclasm, their cult of passion, and their faulty sense of duty, with denunciation and satire. In her *Strictures on the Modern System of Female Education* Hannah More condemns novels of the school of Rousseau:

They teach ... that no duty exists that is not prompted by feeling; that impulse is the main-spring of virtuous actions. ... Alas! they do not know that the best creature of impulse that ever lived, is but a wayward, unfixed, unprincipled being! That the best *natural* man requires a curb.... (*Works*, vol. 1: *Strictures*, chap. 1, p. 318)

[15] Similar encomiums of sensibility and condemnations of social abuses are found in Mary Wollstonecraft's posthumously published *The Wrongs of Women* (1798) and in Mary Hays's *The Victim of Prejudice* (1799).

Maria Edgeworth devoted a short novel entitled "Angelina" (1801) to satire of the romantic-revolutionary novelists. "Angelina," whose real name is Anne Warwick, leads a lonely life in the household of her guardian, Lady Diana Chillingworth. She takes to reading novels, and enters into a correspondence with a female novelist of the romantic-revolutionary school who calls herself "Araminta." Under the influence of Araminta's pernicious doctrines, Angelina decides that her guardian has no claims on her filial duty, and resolves to run away from home and join her new friend. Fortifying herself with Araminta's jargon about independence and firmness of mind, and providing herself with a properly heroic name, she writes to Lady Diana:

> It is my *unalterable determination* to *act* and *think* upon every occasion for myself; though I am well aware that they who start out of the common track, either in words or action, are exposed to the ridicule and persecution of vulgar or illiberal minds. They who venture to carry the *first* torch into *unexplored* or *unfrequented* passages in the mine of truth are exposed to the most imminent danger. Rich, however, are the treasures of the place, and cowardly the soul that hesitates! . . . I am not unmindful of the kindness I have received from your ladyship. It has not been without a *painful* struggle that I have broken my bonds asunder— the bonds of what is *falsely* called *duty*: *spontaneous* gratitude will ever have full, *indisputable, undisputed* power over the heart and *understanding* of
> ANNE-ANGELINA WARWICK
> (*Tales and Novels*, vol. 1, "Angelina," p. 228)

Eventually, after a series of unpleasant and disillusioning adventures, Angelina comes under the influence of a sensible and kindly older woman, Lady Frances Somerset, and exposure to the older woman's good sense and good principles causes her to reform.

A similar work, and one that is particularly interesting because of some points in which it closely resembles *Persuasion*, is Elizabeth Hamilton's satire entitled *Memoirs of Modern Philosophers* (1800). The novel has two sets of characters, the "modern philosophers," who read the "novels and metaphysics" of the school of Rousseau and Godwin and absorb their doctrines, and the virtuous Christians. The "heroine" of the *Memoirs* is Bridgetina Botherim, a cruel caricature of Mary Hays, who fancies herself an enlightened soul although she is stupid and ignorant, and a romantic heroine although she is crippled and ugly. Julia Delmond is a beautiful, sensitive girl who has been similarly corrupted. And there is Mr. Vallaton, a scoundrel who uses "modern philosophy" to justify unprincipled behavior. The chief exponents of conservatism are Harriet Orwell, her father Dr. Orwell, and her aunt, Miss Goodwin; Henry Sidney and his father, Mr. Sidney; and Mrs. Fielding, a long-time friend and onetime sweetheart of Mr. Sidney. The modern philosophers are admirers of strength of mind and strength of feeling. "'It is great passions that bespeak great powers, and great powers are but another expression for great energies, and in great energies the whole of virtue is comprised,'"[16] Vallaton declares. They denounce religion, filial piety, and all else that tends, in their opinions, to confine the free spirit. Bridgetina Botherim sets out, in the manner of Emma Courtney, to persuade a young man to

[16] Elizabeth Hamilton, *Memoirs of Modern Philosophers* (London, 1801), vol. 1, chap. 9, p. 74. All references are to this edition. Jane Austen describes Mrs. Hamilton as "a respectable writer" in a letter of November 6, 1813 (*Letters*, p. 372).

love her, and the results are ludicrous. The story of Julia Delmond, however, is tragic in its consequences. Vallaton persuades Julia that he is in love with her. He undermines her religious beliefs and convinces her "'that the prejudices of *filial duty*, and *family affection, gratitude to benefactors*, and *regard to promises*, are the great barriers to the state of perfect virtue'" (vol. 2, chap. 10, p. 280). When her father announces that he intends to allow an eligible young man to pay his addresses to her, Julia decides that she is a victim of parental tyranny. Vallaton, echoing Godwin, urges her to exert her fortitude, to display "'strength and energy to soar above each vulgar prejudice'" (vol. 2, chap. 6, p. 168), and to elope with him:

> "And will you tamely submit to this outrage upon the first principles of justice? Will you, from an immoral and slavish deference to the man who calls himself your father, sacrifice the first rights of humanity—the right of following your own inclination? What magic is there in the name of father, that can sanctify so base a direliction [*sic*] of duty? (vol. 2, chap. 10, p. 274)

Julia does elope with him, he mistreats and deserts her, and she dies a tragic death.

Mrs. Hamilton also has a great deal to say about the modern philosophers' notions of "fortitude" and "strength of mind." "Female fortitude" had always been a popular subject with the more conservative novelists of the day. But their conception of the nature of true fortitude and strength of mind, and of the degree of these qualities that was desirable in a woman, was quite different from that of the romantic-revolutionary novelists. Like Mrs. Williams, in *The Advantages of Education*, the conservative writers "considered fortitude as absolutely necessary in the catalogue of female virtues." [17] But true fortitude, they felt, consisted in self-control rather than in self-assertion, in the ability to restrain one's emotions rather than in the determination to indulge them at all costs. Thus Laura Montreville, the heroine of *Self-Control*, resolves to reject a man she truly loves when she discovers that his morals are bad. Again, in a moment of crisis she saves the life of her hero by remaining cool and administering first aid, rather than giving way to her emotions, when he is wounded. Fanny Burney's Evelina displays the same brand of courage when, fearing that the unfortunate Mr. Macartney is about to commit suicide, she conquers her terrors and seizes his pistols, earning the following accolade from Mr. Villars: "Though gentleness and modesty are the peculiar attributes of your sex, yet fortitude and firmness, when occasion demands them, are virtues as noble and as becoming in women as in men" (p. 237). The conventional heroine usually combines strength of mind with gentleness of temperament in the manner that Mr. Villars' words would suggest to be ideal. Thus Madame de Fleury, the heroine of the short story of that title in Maria Edgeworth's *Tales of Fashionable Life* (1809), after saving a shrieking child from being crippled for life by holding the bones of his broken arm together until a doctor can be brought, is praised as follows:

> From the feminine appearance of this lady, no stranger would have expected such resolution; but with all the natural sensibility and graceful delicacy of her sex, she had none of that weakness or affectation which incapacitates from being useful in real distress. In most sudden accidents, and

[17] Jane West, *The Advantages of Education*, vol. 2, chap. 14, p. 179.

in all domestic misfortunes, female resolution and presence of mind are indispensably requisite: safety, health, and life, often depend upon the fortitude of women. Happy they who, like Madame de Fleury, possess strength of mind united with gentleness of manner and tenderness of disposition! (*Tales and Novels*, vol. 6: "Madame de Fleury," chap. 1, pp. 267–268)

It is this sort of fortitude that Mrs. Hamilton admires, and she forcefully contrasts the fortitude which consists in self-control with the false fortitude that the modern philosophers praise.

One instance of true fortitude is provided in the history of Mrs. Fielding. She and Mr. Sidney were once in love. Mr. Sidney's only chance of obtaining an income sufficient to support a wife, however, lay in accepting a clerical living. He could not conscientiously assent to the articles of the established church; and Mrs. Fielding, in spite of her love for him, urged him to reject the offered living. "An air of heroic fortitude," the reader is told, "mingled with the native meekness and gentleness that characterised her manners," as she renounced him (vol. 2, chap 12, p. 313). Another example of real strength of mind is provided by Harriet Orwell. She and Henry Sidney are deeply in love, but Henry, a struggling young doctor, is poor; like Captain Wentworth in *Persuasion*, he must achieve success in his profession before he can support a wife. Harriet has an aunt, the kindly but prudent Mrs. Goodwin, who serves as her mentor, and Mrs. Goodwin argues, in the manner of Lady Russell, that it would be folly for Henry to encumber himself at this stage in his career, and urges Harriet to reject him. "'I trust,'" she says, "'you have more real virtue, fortitude, and courage, than to shrink from the painful task'" (vol. 2, chap. 4, p. 136). Harriet dismisses Henry, and he goes off to London. Before long, however, he is rich. He resumes his courtship, and he and Harriet are married.[18]

Jane Austen herself was aware of what was called "modern philosophy" and satirized it to some extent in her *Sanditon*. Here Sir Edward Denham, the would-be romantic seducer who hopes to persuade Clara Brereton to elope with him, would seem to have been influenced by the bad language and worse principles of the romantic-revolutionary writers, as well as by "all the impassioned and most exceptionable parts" of Richardson. He thus describes his taste in literature:

> "You will never hear me advocating those puerile Emanations which detail nothing but discordant Principles incapable of Amalgamation, or those vapid tissues of ordinary Occurrences from which no useful Deductions can be drawn.—In vain may we put them into a literary Alembic; —we can distil nothing which can add to Science. . . . The Novels which I approve are such as display Human Nature with Grandeur—such as shew her in the Sublimities of intense Feeling—such as exhibit the progress of strong Passion from the first Germ of incipient Susceptibility to the utmost Energies of Reason half-dethroned—where we see the strong spark of Woman's Captivations elicit such Fire in the Soul of Man as leads him—(though at the risk of some Aberration from the strict line of Primitive Obligations)—to hazard all, dare all, atcheive all, to obtain her. . . . They hold forth the most splendid Portraitures of high Conceptions, Unbounded Veiws, illimitable Ardour, in-

---

[18] Some other novels which attacked "modern philosophy" are Elizabeth Hamilton's *Letters of a Hindoo Rajah* (1796), Isaac D'Israeli's *Vaurien* (1797), Charles Lloyd's *Edmund Oliver* (1798), George Walker's *The Vagabond* (1799), and Charles Lucas' *The Infernal Quixote* (1800).

domptible Decision— . . . These are the Novels which enlarge the primitive Capabilities of the Heart, & which it cannot impugn the Sense or be any Dereliction of the character, of the most anti-puerile Man, to be conversant with." (*Minor Works*, pp. 403–404)

This could serve as a parody of the preface to *The Memoirs of Emma Courtney*, which reads, in part, as follows:

> The most interesting, and the most useful, fictions, are, perhaps, such, as delineating the progress, and tracing the consequences, of one strong, indulged, passion or prejudice, afford materials, by which the philosopher may calculate the powers of the human mind . . . It had commonly been the business of fiction to pourtray characters, not as they really exist, but, as, we are told, they ought to be—a sort of *ideal perfection*, in which nature and passion are melted away, and jarring attributes wonderfully combined.
>
> In delineating the character of Emma Courtney, I had not in view these fantastic models: I meant to represent her as a human being, loving virtue while enslaved by passion. . . . The philosopher—who is not ignorant, that light and shade are more powerfully contrasted in minds rising above the common level; that, as rank weeds take strong root in a fertile soil, vigorous powers not unfrequently produce fatal mistakes and pernicious exertions . . . may, possibly, discover in these Memoirs traces of reflection, and of attention to the phaenomena of the human mind. (Preface, pp. 4–5)

And in a manner worthy of a modern philosopher Sir Edmund defends Burns's deviations from conventional moral standards as the concomitants of his genius:

> "He was all ardour & Truth!—His Genius & his Susceptibilities might lead him into some Aberrations—But who

is perfect?—It were Hyper-criticism, it were Pseudo-philosophy to expect from the soul of high-toned Genius, the grovellings of a common mind.—The Coruscations of Talent, elicited by impassioned feeling in the breast of Man, are perhaps incompatible with some of the prosaic Decencies of Life; . . . nor can any Woman be a fair Judge of what a Man may be propelled to say, write or do, by the soverign impulses of illimitable Ardour." (*Minor Works*, p. 398)

In the unfinished *Sanditon* Jane Austen's response to the notions of the romantic-revolutionaries takes the form of parody. *Persuasion* is a response of another sort to doctrines of the disciples of Rousseau and Godwin.

II

Persuasion is certainly not a satire on *Political Justice* or the *Nouvelle Héloise*. Nevertheless, I think that Jane Austen sees, and intends her readers to see, a resemblance between Captain Wentworth and the character type of the modern philosopher, and that this resemblance suggests a habit of mind that, in her opinion, requires modification. Jane Austen holds that Wentworth, like the romantic-revolutionary novelists, tends too hastily to assume that an ability to control one's feelings is a sign of shallowness, and that a determination to act without regard to anything but the dictates of one's own will is an indication of strength. Wentworth's feelings regarding Anne Elliot's yielding to "persuasion" and breaking her engagement, and the manner in which they are expressed, help to indicate this habit of mind.

In breaking the engagement with Wentworth, Anne is motivated chiefly by two things. Because Lady Russell has been "almost a mother" to her, giving her the affection and care she has failed to receive elsewhere, Anne acquiesces in her judgment that the engagement is a "wrong thing" even though Lady Russell's views are not her own. The second factor in her decision is a desire to act in Wentworth's best interests.

> Lady Russell, whom she had always loved and relied on, could not, with such steadiness of opinion, and such tenderness of manner, be continually advising her in vain. She was persuaded to believe the engagement a wrong thing. ... But it was not a merely selfish caution, under which she acted, in putting an end to it. Had she not imagined herself consulting his good, even more than her own, she could hardly have given him up.—The belief of being prudent, and self-denying principally for *his* advantage, was her chief consolation, under the misery of a parting—a final parting; and every consolation was required, for she had to encounter all the additional pain of opinions, on his side, totally unconvinced and unbending, and of his feeling himself ill-used by so forced a relinquishment. (pp. 27–28)

Ann behaves, in short, in the manner approved by the conservative novelists, sacrificing her inclinations to her sense of right and her duties toward others. Hers is, clearly, the action of a Harriet Orwell. Wentworth, however, sees Anne's behavior in the "persuasion" situation as it would appear to the eyes of the romantic-revolutionary novelists. He takes the broken engagement as an indication that Anne lacks strength of mind and its concomitant, strength of feeling. Anne has given him up out of a weak-minded deference for Lady Russell and her notions of prudence and propriety. If she had really loved him, he feels, she could never have forsaken him—least of all on behalf of an interfering old woman and her notions of what is socially acceptable. To him Anne appears feeble and fickle, incapable of the kind of love he had felt for her. At the beginning of the novel the reader is told that

> he had not forgiven Anne Elliot. She had used him ill; deserted and disappointed him; and worse, she had shewn a feebleness of character in doing so, which his own decided, confident temper could not endure. She had given him up to oblige others. It had been the effect of over-persuasion. (p. 61)

The most detailed expression of Wentworth's views on the broken engagement, however, and the strongest indication of his adherence to beliefs similar to those of the romantic-revolutionary novelists, occurs during his conversation with Louisa Musgrove during the "long walk" to Winthrop (pp. 84–89).

Here, Anne's supposed shallowness is first contrasted with the romantic devotion of the stouthearted Mrs. Croft, who refuses to allow difficulties and dangers of any kind to separate her from her husband. Apropos of Wentworth's mentioning the fact that Mrs. Croft is at this moment probably risking her neck driving with the admiral in his gig, Louisa declares: "'If I loved a man, as she loves the Admiral, I would be always with him, nothing should ever separate us, and I would rather be overturned by him, than driven safely by anybody else!'" "'Had you? . . . I honour you!'" Wentworth replies "with enthusiasm." Then follows Mary Musgrove's attempt to prevent Henrietta Musgrove from visiting Winthrop. On the surface, the incident seems a parallel in miniature to the situation that had existed among Anne, Wentworth, and Lady Russell. Although Henrietta has been momentarily attracted to Wentworth, and Charles has been jealous, they are still in love, and Henrietta's visit to Winthrop will be an indication of her continuing affection for Charles. Mary, who does not consider Charles an eligible suitor for her sister-in-law, is anxious to keep Henrietta from being thrown together with him whenever possible, and she almost succeeds in persuading Henrietta not to go to Winthrop. But Louisa argues for Charles, and Henrietta makes the visit that is to lead to a reconciliation with him and, ultimately, to their marriage. As Anne, who overhears the conversation between Wentworth and Louisa, realizes, Wentworth's remarks are indirectly a commentary on her own behavior in yielding to persuasion. Louisa declares that she would not brook such interference as Mary's in her own affairs:

> "And so, I made her go. I could not bear that she should be frightened from the visit by such nonsense. What!—would I be turned back from doing a thing that I had determined to do, and that I knew to be right, by the airs and interference of such a person? —or, of any person I may say. No,—I have no idea of being so easily persuaded. When I have made up my mind, I have made it. And Henrietta seemed entirely to have made up hers to call at Winthrop today—and yet, she was as near giving it up, out of nonsensical complaisance!"

Wentworth, drawing upon the philosophy and the vocabulary of the romantic-revolutionary school, gives her the kind of answer she is looking for. "'Happy for her,'" he says, "'to have such a mind as yours at hand!'"

> "After the hints you gave just now, which did but confirm my own observations, the last time I was in company with him, I need not affect to have no comprehension of what is

going on. I see that more than a mere dutiful morning-visit to your aunt was in question;—and woe betide him, and her too, when it comes to things of consequence, when they are placed in circumstances, requiring fortitude and strength of mind, if she have not resolution enough to resist idle interference in such a trifle as this. Your sister is an amiable creature; but *yours* is the character of decision and firmness, I see. If you value her conduct or happiness, infuse as much of your own spirit into her, as you can. But this, no doubt, you have been always doing. It is the worst evil of too yielding and indecisive a character, that no influence over it can be depended on.—You are never sure of a good impression being durable. Every body may sway it; let those who would be happy be firm.—Here is a nut," said he, catching one down from an upper bough. "To exemplify,— a beautiful glossy nut, which, blessed with original strength, has outlived all the storms of autumn. Not a puncture, not a weak spot any where.—This nut," he continued, with playful solemnity,—"while so many of its brethren have fallen and been trodden under foot, is still in possession of all the happiness that a hazel-nut can be supposed capable of." Then, returning to his former earnest tone: "My first wish for all, whom I am interested in, is that they should be firm. If Louisa Musgrove would be beautiful and happy in her November of Life, she will cherish all her present powers of mind."

For Wentworth, Anne's sacrifice to duty and affection and Henrietta's weak-mindedness are on a par. He admires the devotion that Mrs. Croft exemplifies, and that Louisa professes to be capable of, and he feels that Anne, like Henrietta, lacks the courage of her inclinations. She is emotionally shallow, and she lacks the all-important "fortitude and strength of mind," "resolution," "decision and firmness," "powers of mind." What he does not realize is that there are distinctions to be made between the situations of Anne and Henrietta, that the relations between Henrietta and Mary Musgrove and those of Anne and Lady Russell are not really comparable. Mary is only Henrietta's sister-in-law, and an unpleasant one at that. She has no long-established claim on Henrietta's love or gratitude, nor has Henrietta any reason to respect her judgment. Mary's objections are founded, not on prudence and real concern for Henrietta and Charles, but on shallow snobbery. But to Wentworth, Mary's meddling and Lady Russell's counsel are alike "idle interference," to be brushed aside by any lover with sufficient "fortitude." And Anne, like Henrietta, has weakly succumbed to the pressures of snobbery and prejudice. Wentworth is to see the error of his beliefs in the course of the novel—and, interestingly enough, he is to see it as a result of Anne's adherence to the code of behavior of the "conventional" heroines of conservative novelists on two other occasions.

During the walk to Winthrop, Louisa Musgrove makes a strong and apparently successful bid for Wentworth's admiration, but at the same time she prepares the way for her downfall. Anne's fortunes, on the other hand, although they appear to be at their lowest ebb as she hears exactly how poor Wentworth's opinion of her is, are actually taking a turn for the better. Immediately after Wentworth's lengthy speech Louisa, annoyed by Mary's officiousness, confides to Wentworth the fact that Charles Musgrove had proposed to Anne, unsuccessfully, before asking Mary to marry him. "'Mary is good-natured enough in many respects,'" Louisa says,

> "but she does sometimes provoke me excessively, by her nonsense and her pride; the Elliot pride. She has a great deal too much of the Elliot pride.—We do so wish that Charles

had married Anne instead.—I suppose you know he wanted
to marry Anne?"

    After a moment's pause, Captain Wentworth said,
"Do you mean that she refused him?"

    "Oh! yes, certainly."

    "When did that happen?"

    "I do not exactly know, for Henrietta and I were at school
at the time; but I believe about a year before he married
Mary. I wish she had accepted him. We should all have
liked her a great deal better; and papa and mamma always
think it was her great friend Lady Russell's doing, that she
did not.—They think Charles might not be learned and
bookish enough to please Lady Russell, and that therefore,
she persuaded Anne to refuse him." (pp. 88–89)

The Musgroves' views of the situation Louisa describes are,
needless to say, incorrect. From his knowledge of Lady
Russell, Wentworth knows that she would have approved
of the suit of a man as eligible as Charles was, and not have
argued against him. The reader knows that Lady Russell
had favored Charles and "lamented" Anne's refusal of "the
eldest son of a man, whose landed property and general
importance, were second, in that country, only to Sir
Walter's" (p. 28), but that "in this case, Anne had left
nothing for advice to do" (p. 29). The situation was a
variant of the classic "persuasion" situation, involving
conflict between the prudential views of a parent and the
very different views of a child regarding a proposed match.
And what Anne has done is once again to follow the line of
conduct approved by the conservative novelists, allowing
Lady Russell a "negative voice" in her affairs, but refusing
to compromise her feelings or conscience by allowing herself to be persuaded into marrying against her inclinations.

This time, however, Wentworth's response to Anne's "conventional" behavior is quite different; in fact her action causes his views of her character to be considerably shaken. He can see that, had Anne been really as shallow and weak-willed as he had supposed her to be, she would now be Mrs. Charles Musgrove. And he begins to suspect that he has been less than just to Anne's feelings and her mind. After Louisa's revelation, as he tells Anne during their Union-Street reconciliation scene, "'I knew to a certainty that you had refused one man, at least, of better pretensions than myself: and I could not help often saying, Was this for me?'" (p. 244). "Only at Uppercross had he learnt to do her justice," the reader is told (p. 242). An even stronger shock to the modern philosopher's ideas, and his feelings about Anne, is provided by the trip to Lyme.

At Lyme, Wentworth sees the folly of his own ideas about "powers of mind" exemplified in Louisa Musgrove, and at the same time learns to appreciate Anne's true strength of character. Louisa, whose naturally independent spirit has been bolstered by her knowledge that Wentworth admires strength of mind, foolishly insists on being jumped from the Cobb a second time. Wentworth attempts to "persuade" her not to make a second jump; but Louisa, "'so eager and so resolute'" as he describes her later, declares "'I am determined I will,'" and he acquiesces. The result of Louisa's "firmness," and Wentworth's support of it, is that Louisa falls and is seriously injured.

Jane Austen's audience would surely have recognized the situation in which Anne is then placed and would have seen her actions at the Cobb as an instance of the sort of "fortitude" praised by the conservative novelists—that fortitude which consists in repressing one's feelings in the interests of others. Anne, retaining her self-control while all the others are overcome, "attending with all the strength and zeal, and thought, which instinct supplied, to Henrietta," trying "to suggest comfort to the others ... to quiet Mary, to animate Charles, to assuage the feelings of Captain Wentworth" (p. 111), supplying salts and giving directions, behaves with the strength of mind that Evelina, Laura Montreville, and Madame de Fleury displayed under similar circumstances. And the worth of this sort of fortitude is not lost on Wentworth. Reflecting on the incident, Anne had wondered whether it might cause Wentworth to reexamine his ideas on the subject of strength of character:

> ... whether it ever occurred to him now, to question the justness of his own previous opinion as to the universal felicity and advantage of firmness of character; and whether it might not strike him, that, like all other qualities of the mind, it should have its proportions and limits. (p. 116)

And she was right. Wentworth learns that true strength of mind consists not in "self-will" but in "steadiness of principle":

> ... till that day, till the leisure for reflection which followed it, he had not understood the perfect excellence of the mind with which Louisa's could so ill bear a comparison; or the perfect, unrivalled hold it possessed over his own. There, he had learnt to distinguish between the steadiness of principle, and the obstinacy of self-will, between the darings of heedlessness and the resolution of a collected mind. There, he had seen every thing to exalt in his estimation the woman he had lost, and there begun to deplore the pride, the folly, the madness of resentment, which had kept him from trying to regain her when thrown in his way. (p. 242)

The moral eye-opening at Lyme brings Wentworth to self-knowledge. He admits that because Anne's dissolution of the engagement did not accord with his own ideas, he had failed to do justice to her motives, to her conceptions of duty and self-sacrifice. "He had been unjust to her merits, because he had been a sufferer from them" (p. 241). In reply to Anne's final defense of Lady Russell and her own actions he confesses to moral blindness. "'I too have been thinking over the past,'" he says, "'and a question has suggested itself, whether there may not have been one person more my enemy even than that Lady? My own self.... I did not understand you. I shut my eyes, and would not understand you, or do you justice'" (p. 247). Now that his blindness is cured, he sees Anne as "perfection itself, maintaining the loveliest medium of fortitude and gentleness" (p. 241)—and it is perhaps significant that he now describes her in language so close to that in which Maria Edgeworth and Fanny Burney praise their "conventional" heroines.

It is incorrect, then, to see Wentworth as the novel's moral ideal and Anne as a character who changes and adopts Wentworth's views in the course of the story. On the contrary, Anne remains, conspicuously and consistently, the exemplar of a code of conduct similar to that of what has been called here the "conservative" novel; and in so doing she causes Wentworth, as he observes her behavior and reflects upon it, to question and qualify his modern philosophy, and ultimately to accept her "conventional" conduct in breaking the engagement. Wentworth must redefine his concepts of fortitude and strength of mind. He must be made to see that self-control and self-denial are as admirable as self-assertion. He must learn that to be "prudent and self-denying" is not necessarily to be cold or weak. He must learn to see Anne's belief that one does not live for oneself alone, that one's life is entwined with those of others toward whom he has duties and responsibilities, as a more generous philosophy than his own unqualified romantic individualism.

III

I must hasten to add, however, that Wentworth is not the only major character in *Persuasion* who is brought from moral blindness to self-knowledge. Lady Russell, the character who is placed opposite Wentworth in *Persuasion*'s antithetical pattern, is also reformed. If Wentworth has erred because of his particular beliefs, Lady Russell, with her "over-anxious caution," has underestimated the value of Wentworth's brilliance and energy and belief in himself, and failed to see that they would lead him quickly to success in his profession. Early in the novel the reader is told that, to Lady Russell, Wentworth's "sanguine temper, and fearlessness of mind . . . only added a dangerous character to himself" during the early stages of their acquaintance (p. 27). At the end of the story, however, she must admit that she had been unjust to him: " . . . because Captain Wentworth's manners had not suited her own ideas she had been too quick in suspecting them to indicate a character of dangerous impetuosity . . ." (p. 249). On the other hand, because Mr. Elliot's prudence and propriety were attractive to her, she has failed to see him for the man that he really is and has favored his suit of Anne. "There is a quickness of perception in some," Jane Austen says, "a nicety in the discernment of character, a natural penetration, in short, which no experience in others can equal, and Lady Russell had been less gifted in this part of understanding than her young friend" (p. 249). Faced with Wentworth's success and the revelation of Mr. Elliot's villainy, Lady Russell is forced to admit "that she had been pretty completely wrong, and to take up a new set of opinions and hopes." But, the reader is told, "she loved Anne better than she loved her own abilities; and when the awkwardness of the beginning was over, found little hardship in attaching herself as a mother to the man who was securing the happiness of her other child" (p. 249).

The lines just cited on Anne's "natural penetration," her "nicety in the discernment of character," are significant. While both Lady Russell and Captain Wentworth are afflicted with moral blindness, Anne is remarkably clear-sighted throughout the novel. She appreciates both Wentworth and Lady Russell, yet sees the crucial defect in each of them. Moreover, she quickly comes to a better understanding of Mr. Elliot's real nature than Lady Russell is able to achieve. Long before Mrs. Smith reveals Mr. Elliot's real nature, Anne has begun to see through him. Again, although Wentworth and his friends are shocked at Captain Benwick's sudden attachment to Louisa Musgrove, Anne proves to have been a better judge of Benwick's character than anyone else. Wentworth and the Harvilles have accepted Benwick's apparently "hopeless agony" at the death of Fanny Harville at its face value. And when he learns that, within a year of Fanny's death, Benwick has transferred his affections to the mentally inferior Louisa Musgrove, Wentworth is horrified: "'A man does not recover from such a devotion of the heart to such a woman!—He ought not—He does not'" (p. 183). But long before Benwick's engagement Anne, in spite of—indeed, as will be shown in a moment, because of—his extreme demonstrations of grief, has suspected that he is "not inconsolable." "She is almost too good for me," Jane Austen once wrote, describing Anne Elliot to Fanny Knight (*Letters*, p. 487, March 23, 1817). The remark is understandable: Anne is the only Austen heroine who is allowed to embody the moral norm of her novel, the only one who, from the beginning to the end of her story, possesses "emotional intelligence."

Anne possesses emotional intelligence because she is a blend of "prudence" and "romance," of Lady Russell's caution and propriety, and Wentworth's different qualities. Her well-balanced temperament makes her suspicious of extremes either of prudence or romance; and this is what makes her see as clearly as she does. It was shown that Anne pierces Mr. Elliot's façade although Lady Russell is taken in by him. Anne suspects him because he is too prudent, too polished, because he never shows strong feelings or warmly maintained convictions:

> Mr. Elliot was rational, discreet, polished—but he was not open. There was never any burst of feeling, any warmth of indignation or delight, at the evil or good of others. This, to Anne, was a decided imperfection. . . . She felt that she could so much more depend upon the sincerity of those who sometimes looked or said a careless or a hasty thing, than of those whose presence of mind never varied, whose tongue never slipped. (p. 161)

On the other hand, she proves to be a better judge of his friend Benwick's character than Captain Wentworth is; and, as her conversation with Benwick on the subject of poetry is designed to show, she questions the depth of his feelings because she is wary of his excessive "bursts of feeling":

> . . . having talked of poetry, the richness of the present age, and gone through a brief comparison of opinion as to

the first-rate poets, trying to ascertain whether *Marmion* or *The Lady of the Lake* were to be preferred, and how ranked the *Giaour* and the *Bride of Abydos*; and moreover, how the *Giaour* was to be pronounced, he shewed himself so intimately acquainted with all the tenderest songs of the one poet, and all the impassioned descriptions of hopeless agony of the other; he repeated, with such tremulous feeling, the various lines which imaged a broken heart, or a mind destroyed by wretchedness, and looked so entirely as if he meant to be understood, that she ventured to hope that he did not always read only poetry . . . and . . . mentioned such works of our best moralists, such memoirs of characters of worth and suffering, as occurred to her at the moment as calculated to rouse and fortify the mind by the highest precepts, and the strongest examples of moral and religious endurances. (pp. 100–101)

To Wentworth, Benwick's emotionalism is admirable; it suits his notions about strength of feeling. But Anne suspects, rightly, that feelings so violently and frequently and publicly expressed may be neither deep nor discriminating. Long before his engagement to Louisa, the reader is told, she felt that he was "not inconsolable . . . any tolerably pleasing young woman who had listened and seemed to feel for him, would have received the same compliment. He had an affectionate heart. He must love somebody" (p. 167).

In smaller things, too, Jane Austen takes pains to show that Anne is a blend of prudence and romance. She combines the best elements of the rival "sets" into which *Persuasion* is divided. She is a lover of nature who prefers Uppercross and Lyme to Bath. She admires the picturesque beauty of Lyme. Faced with the possibility of a removal from Kellynch she "grieves to forego all the influence so sweet and so sad of the autumnal months in the country" (p. 33). Yet she is "more elegant and cultivated" than the

Musgrove set. Highly "accomplished," she translates Italian extempore to Mr. Elliot's admiration and astonishment, and, the reader is told, is "a great deal better than either of the Miss Musgroves" as a musician. Similarly, she dislikes the snobbery and formality of the Bath circle: "'I certainly am proud, too proud to enjoy a welcome which depends so entirely on place,'" she says, arguing on the subject of Bath social life with Mr. Elliot (p. 151). Although she admires the warmheartedness of the Musgrove family, she realizes that the excessive informality of relations between the cottage and the hall at Uppercross is "highly imprudent" and productive of "continual subjects of offense." [19]

Thus, if *Persuasion* is read from the point of view of Jane Austen's contemporaries, Anne Elliot emerges clearly as the moral ideal of the novel and a blend of "art" and "nature." The novel involves, not moral growth in Anne, but moral growth in Wentworth and, to some extent, in Lady Russell. Moreover, just as Anne combines "art" and "nature" in the proper proportions within herself, so does she bring about

[19] As Howard Babb has pointed out, even Anne's characteristic habits of speech indicate the blending of "sense" and "sensibility." According to Babb, "If Anne speaks the clearest sense, she is as likely as not to appeal to emotion: 'Nursing,' she tells Mary, 'does not belong to a man, it is not his province. A sick child is always the mother's property, her own feelings generally make it so' (p. 56). And even when she directs—without real cause—a moral generalization against herself, her vigorous phrasing shows her to be in emotional possession of it: 'What wild imaginations one forms, where dear self is concerned! How sure to be mistaken!' (p. 201). All of these generalizations express reason saturated with Anne's personal feeling thus becoming a verbal echo, as it were, of that union of innate sense with emotional sensitivity which I have called her intuition" (*The Fabric of Dialogue*, p. 216; Babb's page references are to the Oxford edition).

harmony between her modern philosopher and her over-cautious mentor. From being antagonists at the beginning of the novel, Lady Russell and Wentworth, after each has attained self-knowledge, become firm friends through their love for Anne. Lady Russell finds "little hardship in attaching herself as a mother" to Wentworth. Wentworth can soon "value [Lady Russell] from his heart." Far from being Jane Austen's concession to "romance," *Persuasion* embodies the same moral vision found throughout her work —a vision based on her belief in the conception that the good is a harmony of opposites, that all qualities should have proportions and limits.

Afterword

Delight in the complexity of human nature and the subtlety of human relationships provides the most important inspiration for Jane Austen's mature work. Yet in all her novels the sense of life's complexity emerges and is developed in relation to literature. Jane Austen began her literary career with parody and burlesque written for the bookish family circle whose tastes, opinions, and libraries she shared. The mature novels (*Northanger Abbey* with its elements of broad parody must be considered to be in part an exception to this generalization) are not oriented toward the criticism of literature in the same way that so many of her early writings are. Nevertheless, the burlesque writer's habit of relying on and exploiting an audience's familiarity with various kinds of literature persists throughout the later works and remains always an important element in her art. (It is interesting in this respect to note that even in the little that exists of the unfinished *Sanditon* Clara Brereton and Sir Edward Denham are being conceived in relation to the traditional materials of fiction.) These essays have attempted to examine some of the manifestations of Jane Austen's habit of communicating in terms of recognizably conventional materials.

The manifestations are many and varied; in the course

of the preceding series of discussions, a number of relationships, differing in both degree and kind, have been observed between the materials in Jane Austen's novels and the analogues they suggest. *Northanger Abbey, Sense and Sensibility,* and *Emma,* for instance, are novels that are related quite closely and in detail to certain kinds of stories. They follow almost point-by-point (albeit ironically at some points) the patterns of the sorts of works that they resemble. *Pride and Prejudice, Mansfield Park,* and *Persuasion,* on the other hand, while they involve certain recognizable character types, situations and ideas, are somewhat more loosely related to the fictional and didactic literature that they would have been likely to recall to the minds of Jane Austen's early nineteenth-century readers. Again, in the handling of their materials *Northanger Abbey, Sense and Sensibility,* and *Emma* make use of a similar technique, a sort of definition-by-contrast. *Northanger Abbey* follows the traditional formula associated with what has been referred to as the "young lady's introduction to the world," but at a certain point emphatically departs from it to become an open, name-dropping criticism of the novelists from whom Jane Austen borrows the formula, and an assertion of her own quite different moral vision. *Sense and Sensibility* and, especially, *Emma* are considerably more subtle in their definitions-by-contrast, but are nevertheless fairly closely related to *Northanger Abbey* in the techniques they employ with their materials. In *Sense and Sensibility* Jane Austen follows closely and at length the pattern of other "sense and sensibility" stories such as those of Maria Edgeworth and Mrs. Jane West, but in at least two places she deliberately makes her novel the reverse of what an audience that shared her literary milieu would have expected to find in such stories, and dramatizes the differences between her own fallible "sensible sister" and those found in works like *A Gossip's Story* or *The Advantages of Education* or "Mademoiselle Panache." *Emma* uses the pattern of the "female Quixote" novels that have been discussed, combining it with elements of the "mock-heroine" stories to produce a magnificently complicated blend of the materials of antiromance that helps to condemn some of Emma Woodhouse's romantic notions. But the novel also turns upon the works that it resembles, and in ultimately following, in a modified form, the patterns of "real" romance, presents a richer, subtler vision of life than the works of writers such as Barrett, Crabbe, and Charlotte Lennox embody. In *Mansfield Park* and *Persuasion*, on the other hand, Jane Austen does not turn upon her fellow authors in the same way. (Fanny Price, the traditional antitype to the "accomplished" woman, is criticized somewhat in *Mansfield Park*; but, as noted earlier, Jane Austen's audience would not see Fanny's displays of a bookishly naïve outlook on life as things reflecting on features of the tradition represented by Hannah More's and Maria Edgeworth's works.) In discussing *Mansfield Park* and *Persuasion* I have been chiefly concerned with identifying similarities to certain other works and using these similarities as bases for what are perhaps more accurate and sympathetic interpretations than one sometimes meets with. *Pride and Prejudice*, finally, operates in yet another way, for it at first impresses the reader with its marked and humorous dissimilarity to works in the tradition of Fanny Burney's *Evelina* and Richardson's *Sir Charles Grandison*, but ultimately takes on some significant resemblances to them.

On the whole, however, this study is concerned not with multiplying distinctions among Jane Austen's works but with emphasizing their essential similarity with respect to their handling of traditional materials. It is, I hope, evident at this point that in each of the six novels that have been discussed traditional material, artfully manipulated, is playing an important part in the intellectual-artistic structure of the work. And in the case of each of the novels, attempts to re-create the probable responses of an early nineteenth-century audience to "borrowed" material and the way it is handled illuminate Jane Austen's thought or art, or both. This illumination, I believe, justifies the treatment of her habit of "borrowing" as an art of allusion.

Acknowledgments

I am happy to be able to acknowledge my debt to professors Reuben Brower and Douglas Bush, of Harvard University, who guided my graduate studies on Jane Austen and whose good counsel was valuable to me. My thanks are due also to Professor Brooke Peirce, of Goucher College, and Mrs. Peirce, for their rigorous and helpful criticism of the manuscript of this book. Parts of my work on Jane Austen were carried on with the assistance of fellowships provided by the University of Nebraska's Research Council, and I am most grateful for the Research Council's generosity.

Index

Babb, Howard, 19 n., 44 n., 94 n., 177 n., 222 n.
Barrett, Eaton Stannard, *The Heroine*, 160, 164–166
Bennet, Agnes Maria, *Ellen, Countess of Castle Howell*, 25
Booth, Wayne C., 156 n., 177 n.
Bradbrook, F. W., 25 n., 89 n., 90 n., 106 n., 125 n., 147 n., 149 n., 155, 155 n., 178 n.
Brontë, Charlotte, 12
Brooke, Frances, *Lady Julia Mandeville*, 46, 178
Brower, Reuben, 90 n., 94 n.
Brunton, Mary, *Self-Control*, 46 n., 195, 204
Brydges, Egerton, *Mary de Clifford*, 90 n.
Burney, Fanny, 23–24; *Cecilia*, 81–82, 95–96; *Evelina*, 83–84, 90–93, 204
Burney, Sarah, *Clarentine*, 159

Chapman, R. W., 81 n., 113 n., 115 n., 126 n., 190 n., 193 n.

Charlton, Mary, *Rosella*, 161 n.
"Courtney, Mrs.," *Isabinda of Bellefield*, 178 n.
Cowper, William, *The Task*, 149 n.
Crabbe, George, " Ellen Orford " in *The Borough*, 161–162

Daiches, David, 75 n.
Dalziel, Margaret, 195 n.
Day, Thomas, *Sanford and Merton*, 111
Dickens, Charles, *Bleak House*, 178 n.
D'Israeli, Isaac, *Vaurien*, 206 n.
Drew, Philip, 94 n.
Duffy, Joseph M., 190 n.
Duncan-Jones, E. E., 55 n., 77 n., 86 n., 178 n.

Edgeworth, Maria, " Angelina," 161 n., 201–202; *Belinda*, 47 n.; "Madame de Fleury," 204–205; "Mademoiselle Panache," Part I, 47–50; Part II, 116–117; *Patronage*, 47 n.

231

Edinburgh Review, 47, 112–113
Eliot, George, *Daniel Deronda*, 136
Emden, C. S., 31 n.

Fleishman, Avrom, 122 n., 130 n., 149 n.

Gilpin William, *Observations on the Mountains and Lakes of Cumberland and Westmorland*, 106 n.
Gisbourne, Thomas, *Enquiry into the Duties of the Female Sex*, 113, 195
Godwin, William, *Political Justice*, 196
Griffin, Cynthia, 19 n.

Hamilton, Elizabeth, *Letters of a Hindoo Rajah*, 206 n.; *Memoirs of Modern Philosophers*, 161 n., 202–206; *Popular Essays*, 113
Hays, Mary, *Memoirs of Emma Courtney*, 197–198, 207; *Victim of Prejudice*, 200 n.
Helme, Elizabeth, *Duncan and Peggy*, 25
Hughes, E. N., 156 n.
Hughes, R. E., 184 n.
Hull, Thomas, *History of Sir William Harrington*, 85, 86 n., 106 n.

Inchbald, Elizabeth, *Simple Story*, 46

Johnson, R. Brimley, 28 n., 55 n., 81, 142, 187 n.
Johnson, Samuel, 25 n., 125 n.

Kearful, Frank J., 39 n.
Kennedy, Margaret, 148 n.
Kliger, Samuel, 75 n.

Lascelles, Mary, 19 n., 40–41, 145 n., 156, 156 n., 161 n., 173, 181
Leavis, Q. D., 90 n., 97 n., 119 n.
Lennox, Charlotte, *Female Quixote*, 162–164
Lerner, Laurence, 177 n.
Litz, A. Walton, 33 n., 39 n., 43 n.
Lloyd, Charles, *Edmund Oliver*, 206 n.
Lucas, Charles, *Infernal Quixote*, 206 n.

McCann, Charles J., 94 n.
McKillop, Alan D., 55 nn., 96 n.
Martin, W. R., 187 n.
Mason, John, *Self-Knowledge*, 8–9, 14 n.
Mathison, John K., 39 n.
Melander, Martin, 54 n.
Moler, Kenneth L., 58 n., 81 n., 86 n.
More, Hannah, *Coelebs in Search of a Wife*, 115–116; *Practical Piety*, 7–8; *Strictures on the Modern System of Female Education*, 113–115, 132–133, 200
Mudrick, Marvin, 43, 71 n., 105 n., 109 n., 130 n., 156 n.

Murrah, Charles, 149 n.
Murray, James Gregory, 177 n.

O'Connor, Frank, 155 n., 187 n.
Otway, Thomas, *Venice Preserved*, 178 n.

Parsons, Eliza, *Mysterious Warning*, 18 n., 194
Porter, Anna Maria, *Lake of Killarney*, 85, 86 n.

Radcliffe, Ann, *Castles of Athlin and Dunbayne*, 22; *Mysteries of Udolpho*, 24–25, 147 n.; *Romance of the Forest*, 158–159
Richardson, Samuel, *Clarissa*, 77; *Pamela*, 77; *Sir Charles Grandison*, 77–81, 105–107, 193–194
Robinson, Mary, *Vancenza*, 159
Roche, Regina Maria, *Children of the Abbey*, 25, 60, 158; *Clermont*, 159–160
Rousseau, Jean-Jacques, *Emile*, 111; *Nouvelle Héloise*, 197

Schneider, Sister M. Lucy, 149 n.
Schorer, Mark, 177 n.
Scott, Walter, *Lay of the Last Minstrel*, 149 n.
Shannon, Edgar F., 175 n.

Smith, Charlotte, *Emmeline*, 161; *Ethelinde*, 55
Southam, B. C., 59 n., 96 n., 100 n.
Spectator, 8

Ten Harmsel, Henrietta, 39 n., 46 n., 55 n., 77 n., 96 n., 98 n., 100 n., 128 n., 130 n., 145 n.
Tompkins, J. M. S., 51 n., 53–54, 55 n., 96 n., 195 n.
Trilling, Lionel, 3–5, 39 n., 109 n., 130 n., 156, 156 n., 175 n.

Van Ghent, Dorothy, 11–12, 75 n.

Watt, Ian, 59
Welpley, W. S., 81 n.
West, Jane, *Advantages of Education*, 56–57, 64, 194, 203–204; *Alicia de Lacy*, 47 n.; *Gossip's Story*, 50–53; *Letters to a Young Lady*, 178
White, Edward M., 178 n.
Wollstonecraft, Mary, *Mary: A Fiction*, 178 n., 198–200; *Wrongs of Women*, 200 n.
Woolf, Virginia, 129, 187 n.
Wright, Andrew, 39 nn., 46 n., 126 n.